GW00420620

Basic

PROMO

BASIC PROMO
Copyright 2012
INDEX BOOK, SL
Consell de Cent, 160 local 3
08015 Barcelona
T +34 93 454 5547
F +34 93 454 8438
ib@indexbook.com
www.indexbook.com

Publisher: Sylvie Estrada
Design: Federica Sala
ISBN: 978-84-92643-90-5

Printed in China.

Basic

PROMO

Pages

To Connect

To Celebrate

To Invite

To Sell

Final Directory

To Connect
006 - 069

001/
Albertini Romain • *CLUB BLISTER is a London- and Paris-based collective of DJs, designers, musicians and promoters.*

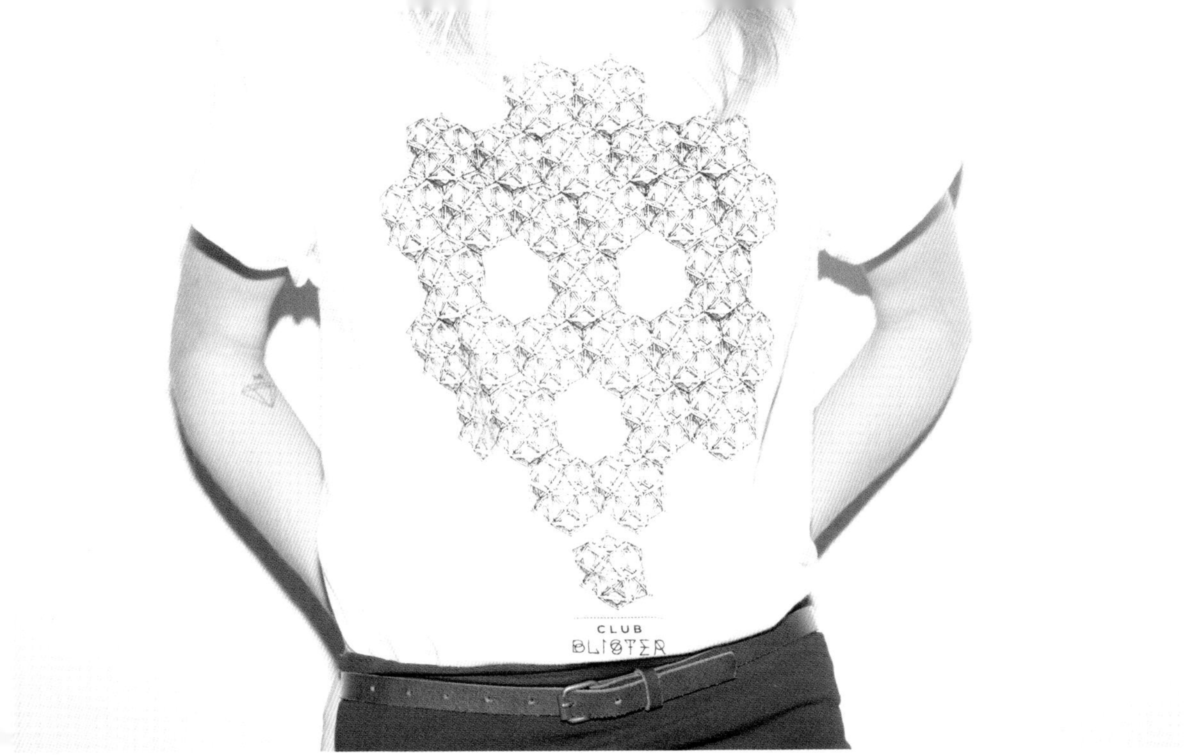
CLUB
BLISTER

CLUB
BLISTER

002/

Claudia Dionne/Ibo Angulo • *Handmade press kit: the idea is for the style, creativity and inspirations linked to the concept to jump out to its readers.*

01 OCT 2009
20 OCT 2009
08 NOV 2009
perro-de-mundo
sueter
juguete
bandana
F. Menta/Tea tree

PLAY
NOTE BOOK

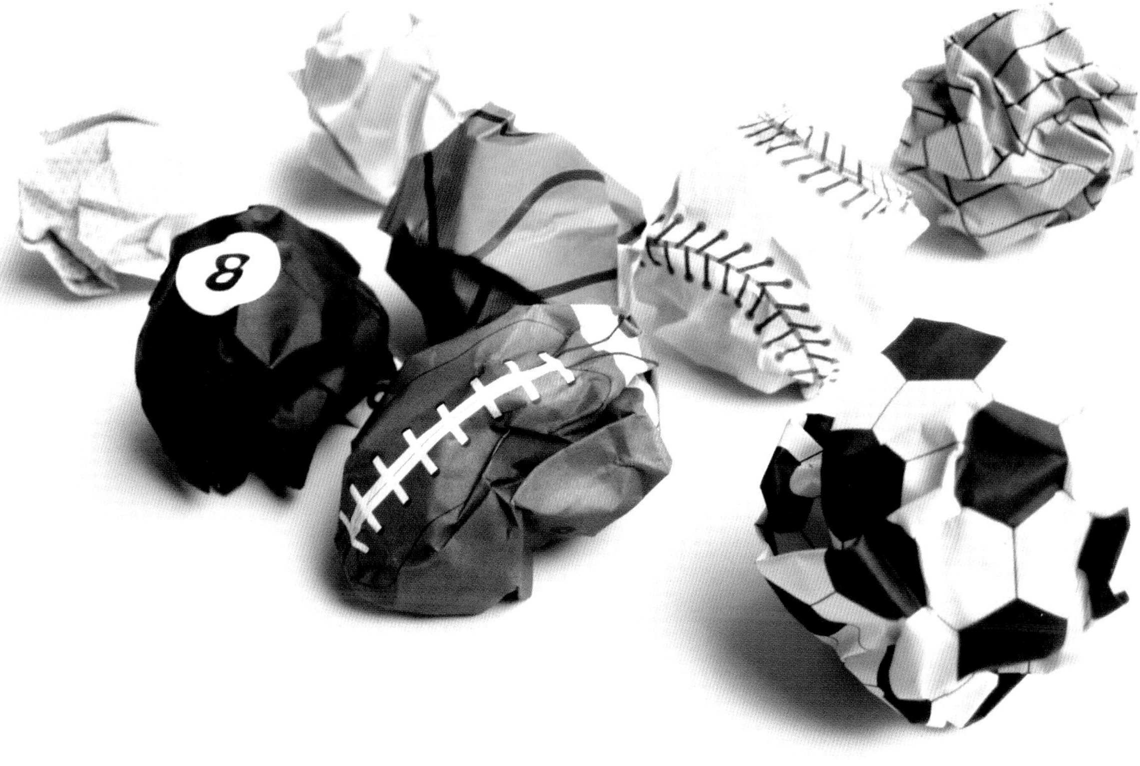

003/
Trapped in Suburbia • *We wanted to get our clients moving behind their desks, so we created this notebook with writing space on one side and patterns from different balls on the other. Just attach a piece of paper to a ball and you can play soccer or rugby, or you can throw a tennis ball in your waste basket.*

004/
Foreign Policy Design Group • *Calendar/Announcement card.*

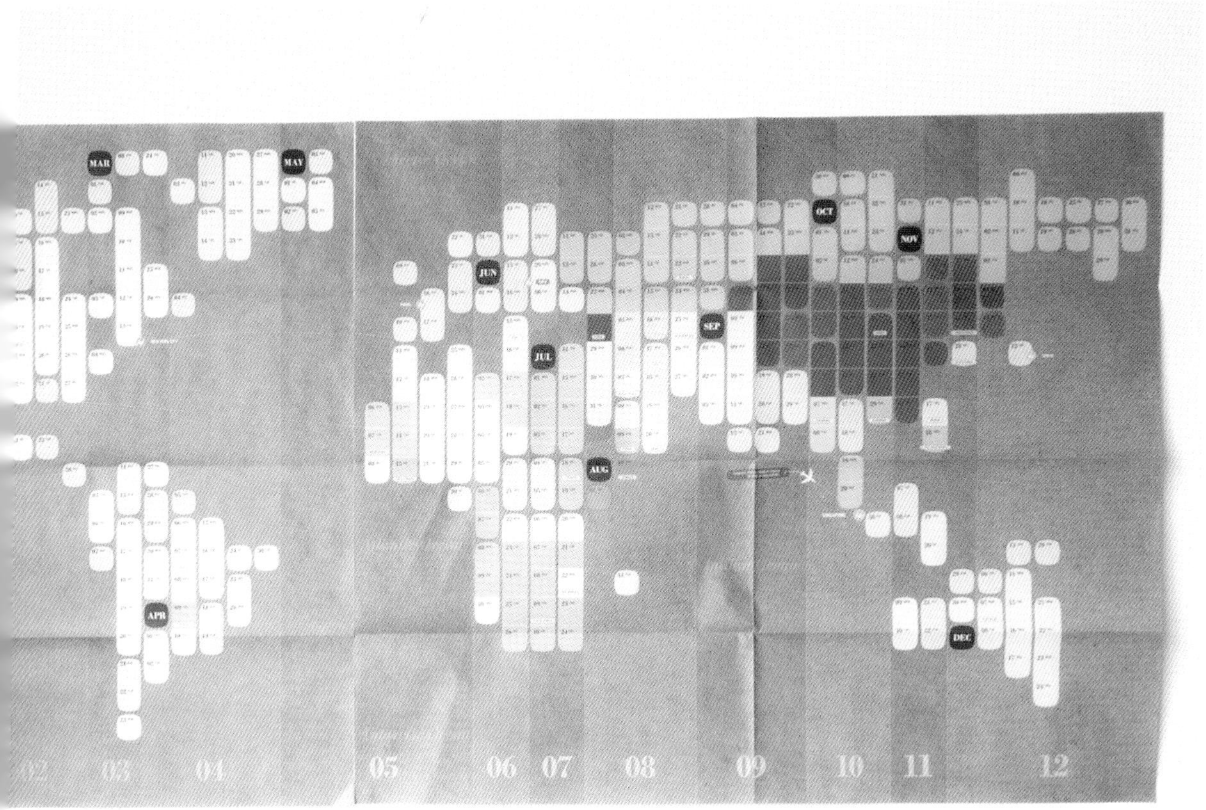
MAR
MAY
JUN
JUL
AUG
SEP
OCT
NOV
APR
DEC
02 03 04 05 06 07 08 09 10 11 12

005/

Pepe Gimeno - Proyecto Gráfico • *In order to promote and disclose how they work, the Habitat Tendencies' Observer provides training materials such as 'WAKE UP!'.*

WAKE
UP!
Taller creativo • Nuevas formas de habitar

Hogar
¿En quién piensas?
Empresa
El día a día

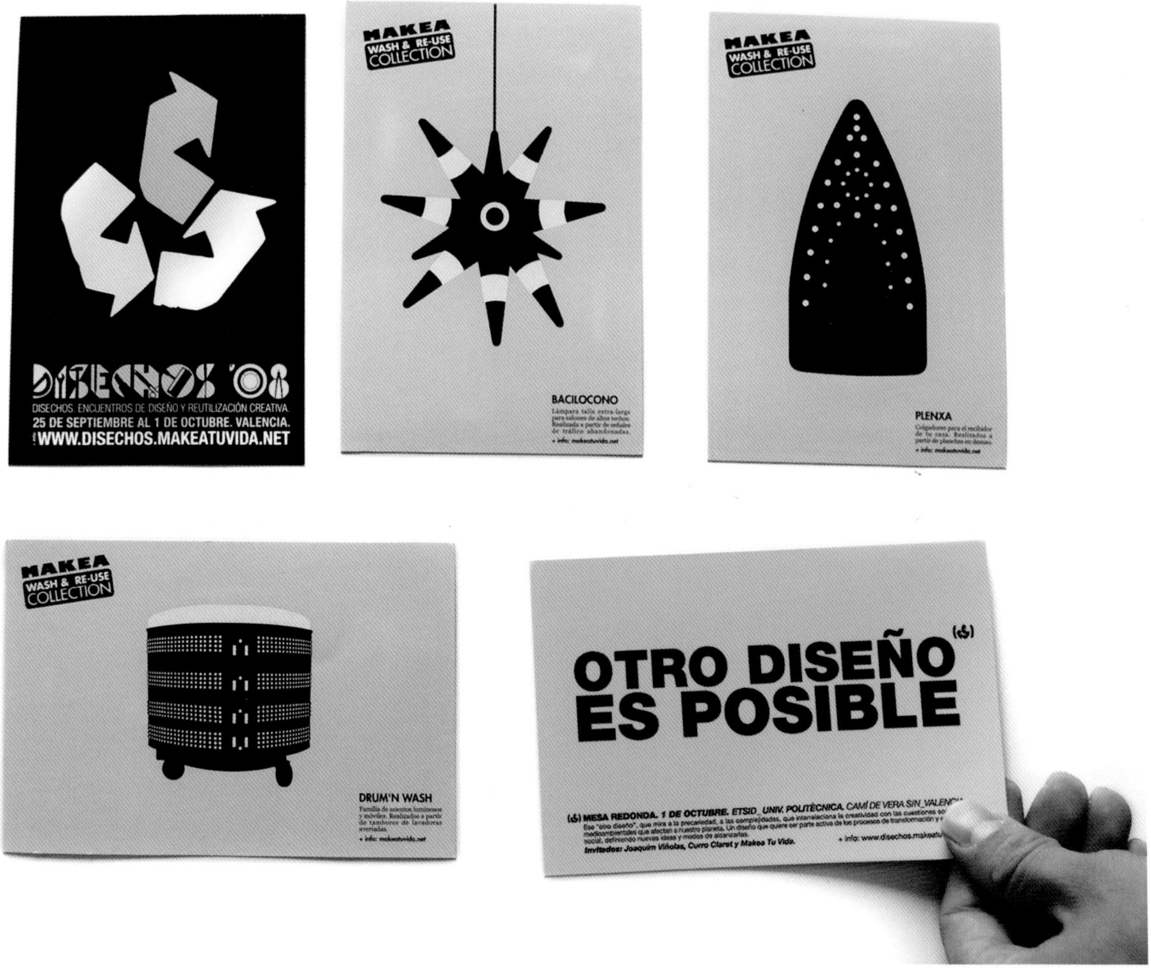

006/
Flou Flou - disoñadores asociados • *2008 materials for 'Disechos', an annual meeting that allows for temporary spaces of dialogue, reflection and work, using creative and technical disciplines.*

007/
MadeThought • *Promotional bag for 'Design Miami Basel' show.*

008/
la regadera grafica | Albert Terré • *To promote the nougat and pure melting chocolate festival with aprons.*

7
JOKER
Joker
ATIPUS.COM
JOKER
Viatges
ESTIU
ATIPUS.COM
viatges d'estiu!
ATIPUS.COM
viatges d'estiu!
RECORRE EL MÓN SENCER
EN 22 DIES
OFERTES!!!
D'ÚLTIM MOMENT
MÉS INFORMACIÓ A
WWW.ATIPUS.COM/ESTIU2010
POKER CARDS
VIATGES D'ESTIU!
ACOMPANYA EL TEU VIATGE AMB
EL MILLOR JOC D'ESTIU
SAFARI PLATJA MUNTANYA CIUTAT
02-24 D'AGOST
TANQUEM PER VACANCES

009/
ATIPUS • *To announce to the clients the days that the studio will be closed for the holidays ATIPUS has created some illustrations that evoke summer travels.*

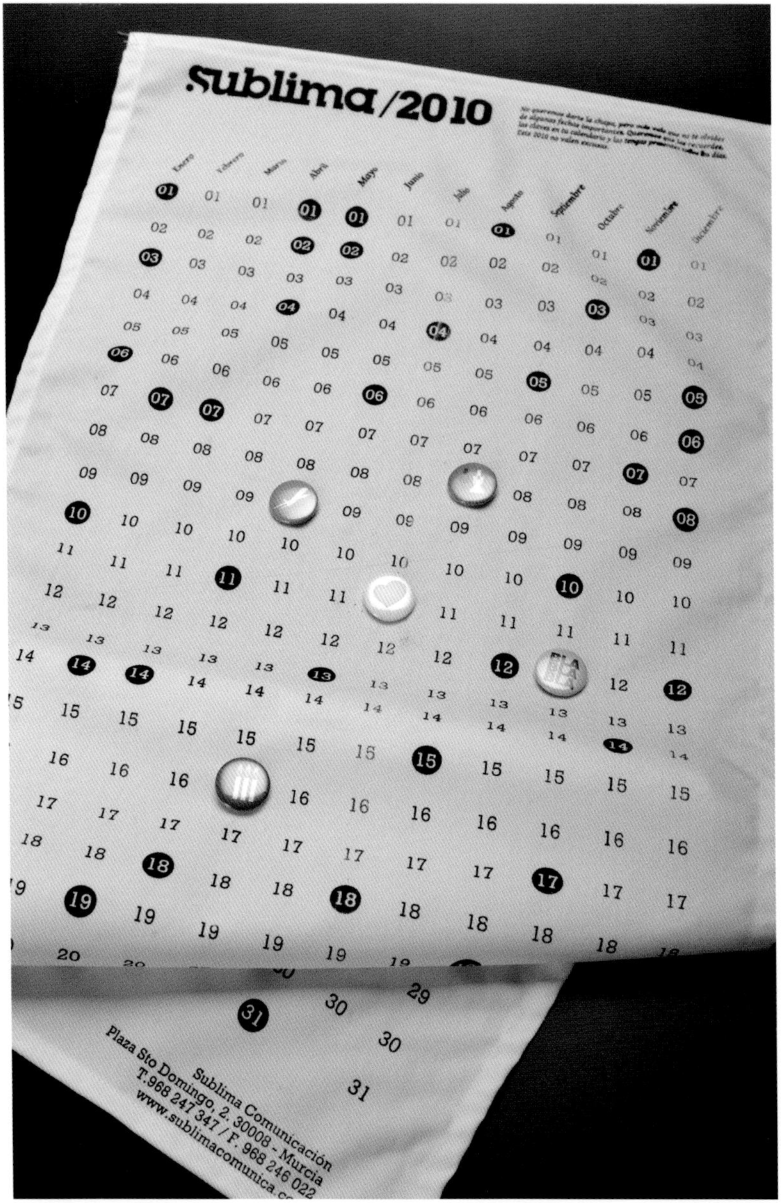

010/
Sublima Comunicación • *Self-promotional calendar on fabric with buttons to point out dates.*

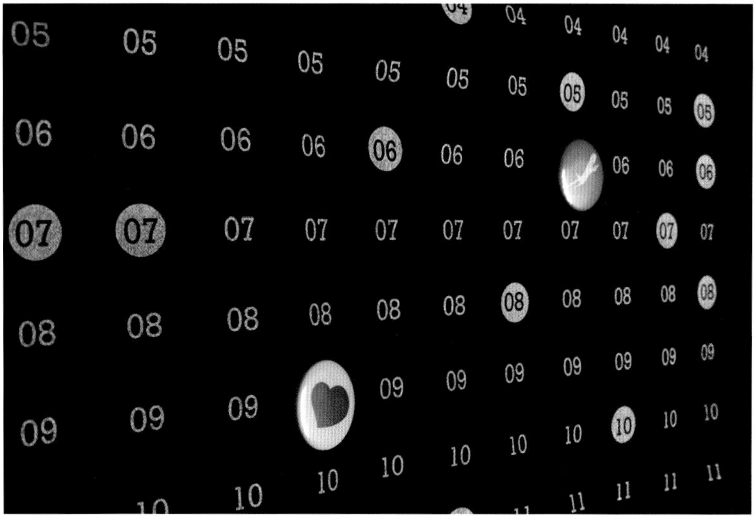
05 05 05 05 05 05 05 05 05 05 05
06 06 06 06 06 06 06 06 06 06
07 07 07 07 07 07 07 07 07 07 07
08 08 08 08 08 08 08 08 08 08 08
09 09 09 09 09 09 09 09 09 09
10 10 10 10 10 10 10 10 10
11 11 11 11

sublima/2010
sublim
BLA
BLA

011/
Raúl Iglesias Design • *Promotional poster mailed to studios and potential clients. It plays on the phrase 'Use me to relax' and is covered in bubble wrap. It contains a shortened version of my CV, including relevant information and a selection of some of my projects.*

ME
RELAX
A little piece of heaven

Ice Cube Type
La tipografía fue creada como parte de un proyecto llamado "Descongelando Ideas" con el objetivo de representar ideas mantenidas en la mente que con el tiempo son rechazadas y desaparecen.
The Ice Cube Type was created as part of a project called "Unfreezing ideas", aimed at representing ideas held in the mind which are eventually rejected and disappear.
Typography and Coffee
Diez y media de la mañana, un poquito de café y un desayuno con tipografía. Sin duda una buena manera de comenzar la mañana. Tener un buen día!!!
Half pass ten in the morning, a bit of coffe and breakfast with typography. The best way to star your day. Have a nice one!
Layers Magazine
People Are Strange

012/
Bunch • *The project evolved from Bunch being chosen to devise a distinct identity for 'The Star of Bethnal Green' in 2008. A traditional long-tailed star was taken and illustrated to create artwork that represented the corresponding month. This was applied each month for approximately a year with all of the illustration done in house by Bunch.*

WalesEvans
Private View
Tuesday 25 5 2010
1–3 Rivington St, London EC2
Exhibition stays open
24 – 28 5 2010
www.bunchofstars.com
by Bunch

by Bunch
In Bunch
IndonesiaHaryoto
NetherlandsHandiedan
RussiaFlakonkishochki
SerbiaPešić
SpainGaliana
SwitzerlandChinof
UgandaMwase
USACassetti
WalesEvans

Hong KongLau
IcelandHafsteinsson
IndonesiaHaryoto
NetherlandsHandiedan
RussiaFlakonkishochki
SerbiaPešić
SpainGaliana

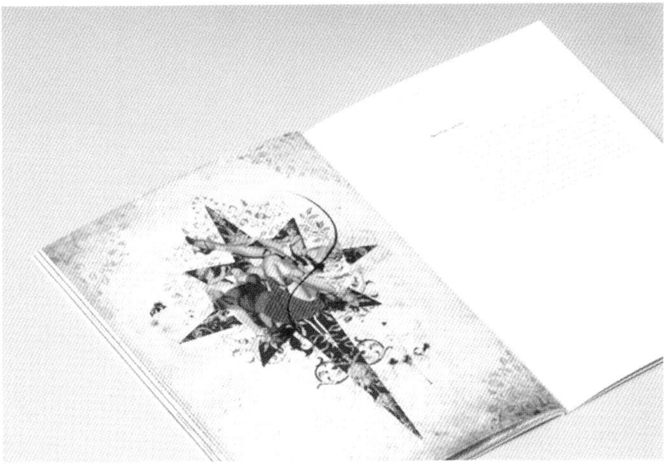

GENERAL INSURANCE ASSOCIATION
A MOST ACCOMPLISHED YEAR
With Thanks To All GIA Contributors In 2009

013/
&Larry • *This calendar was produced for the participants of the Talent Outreach Project. As a year-end promotional gift, it serves dual functions: one side acts a calendar, and the other side pays tribute to contributors for their year-long support.*

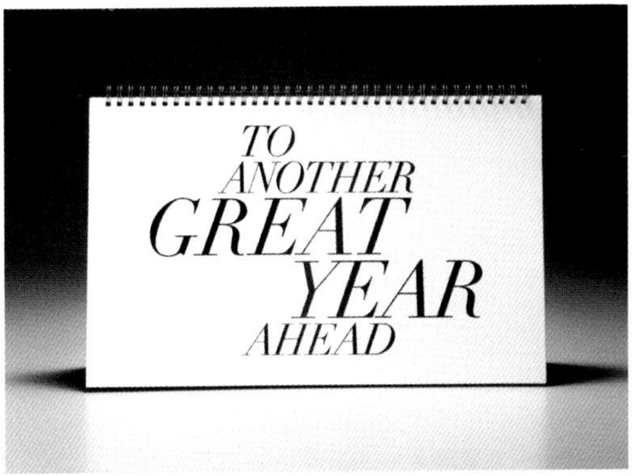
TO
ANOTHER
GREAT
YEAR
AHEAD

02
FEBRUARY
CHINESE NEW YEAR
CHINESE NEW YEAR
CHINESE NEW YEAR

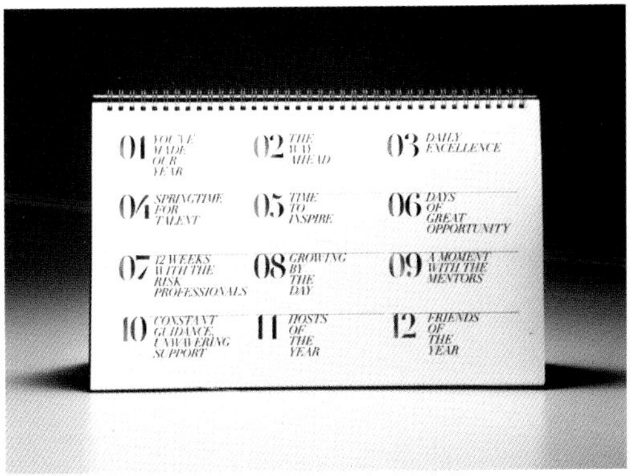
01 YOU'VE MADE OUR YEAR
02 THE WAY AHEAD
03 DAILY EXCELLENCE
04 SPRINGTIME FOR TALENT
05 TIME TO INSPIRE
06 DAYS OF GREAT OPPORTUNITY
07 12 WEEKS WITH THE RISK PROFESSIONALS
08 GROWING BY THE DAY
09 A MOMENT WITH THE MENTORS
10 CONSTANT GUIDANCE, UNWAVERING SUPPORT
11 HOSTS OF THE YEAR
12 FRIENDS OF THE YEAR

03
DAILY EXCELLENCE
A continuous effort to attract, develop and retain talent for the growth and renewal of our industry
MARK LIM

014/
Kanella • *Happy and Sweet. A set of 12 chocolates inspired by the corresponding12 months of the year. It works as a calendar… and each chocolate has to be eaten at the end of the corrisponding month.*

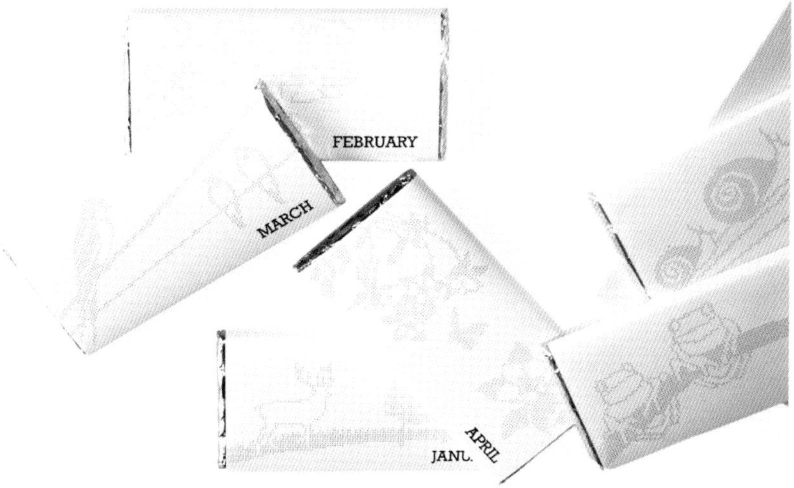
FEBRUARY
MARCH
APRIL

FEBRUARY

Jorge Lorenzo
Hojas de calendario 2010

Junio
L M X J V S D
1 2 3 4 5 6
7 8 9 10 11 12 13
14 15 16 17 18 19 20
21 22 23 24 25 26 27
28 29 30
Mayo
L M X J V S D
1 2
3 4 5 6 7 8 9
10 11 12 13 14 15 16
17 18 19 20 21 22 23
24 25 26 27 28 29 30
31
Marzo
L M X J V S D
1 2 3 4 5 6 7
8 9 10 11 12 13 14
15 16 17 18 19 20 21
22 23 24 25 26 27 28
29 30 31
Diciembre
L M X J V S D
1 2 3 4 5
6 7 8 9 10 11 12
13 14 15 16 17 18 19
20 21 22 23 24 25 26
27 28 29 30 31
Octubre
L M X J V S D
1 2 3
4 5 6 7 8 9 10
11 12 13 14 15 16 17
18 19 20 21 22 23 24
25 26 27 28 29 30 31
Abril
L M X J V S D
1 2 3 4
5 6 7 8 9 10 11
12 13 14 15 16 17 18
19 20 21 22 23 24 25
26 27 28 29 30

015/
Jorge Lorenzo Diseño y Comunicación Visual, S.L. • *Self-promotional calendar.*

016/

Esther Barniol / Projectes Creatius • *Each time a dish is brought to the table, the server also provides the name of the dish on a die-cut circle. At the end of the meal, the customer may take all the circles to remember what he or she ate.*

Josep Xandri

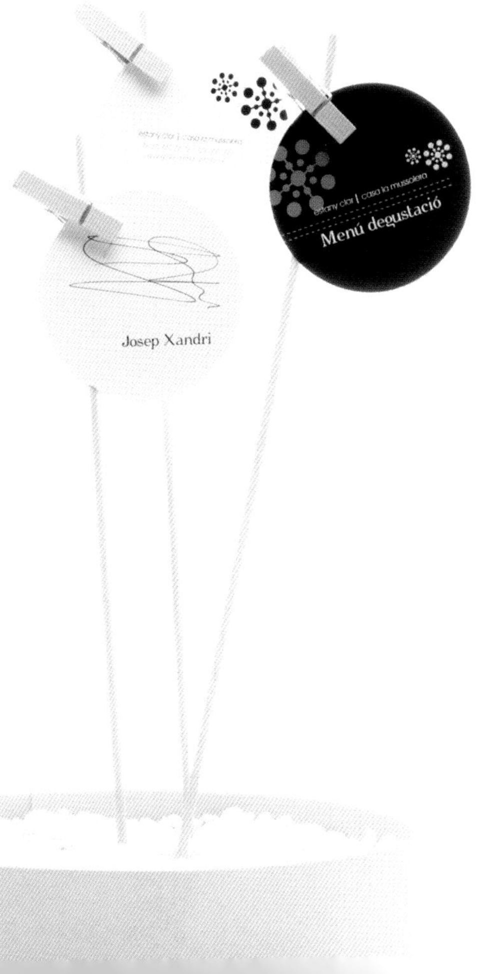
estany clar | casa la mussolera
Menú degustació
Josep Xandri

017/
Toben • *Limited edition calendar that was produced for Toben's launch in January 2010.*

JUL
07
SAT SUN
06

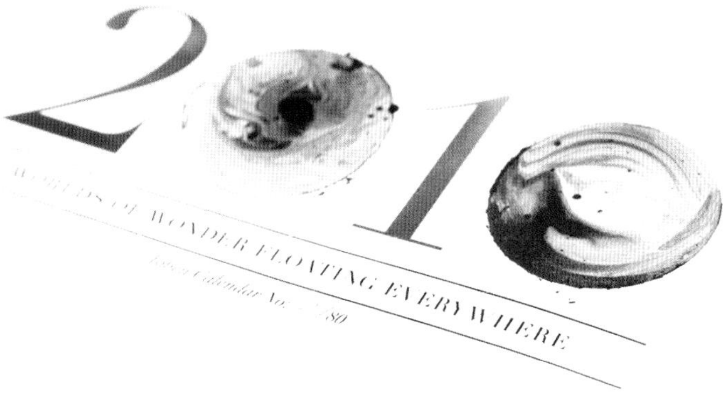
2010
WONDER FLOWING EVERYWHERE

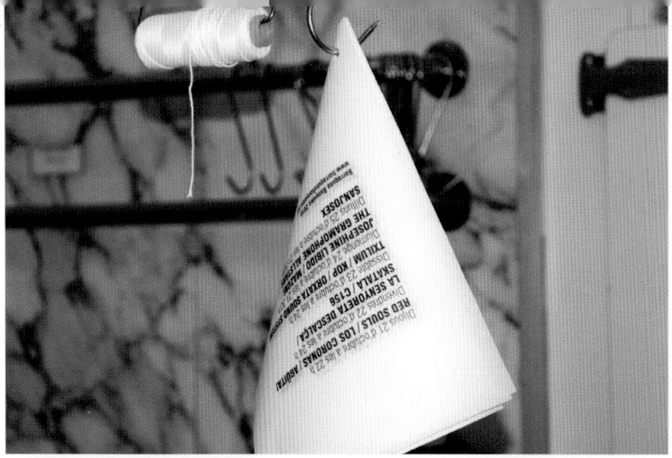

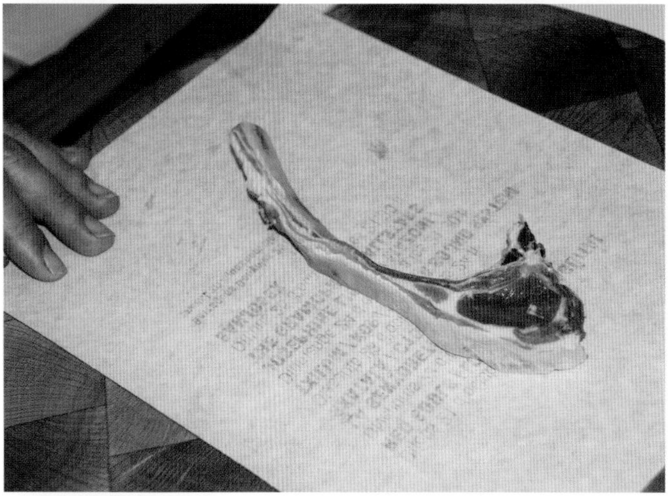

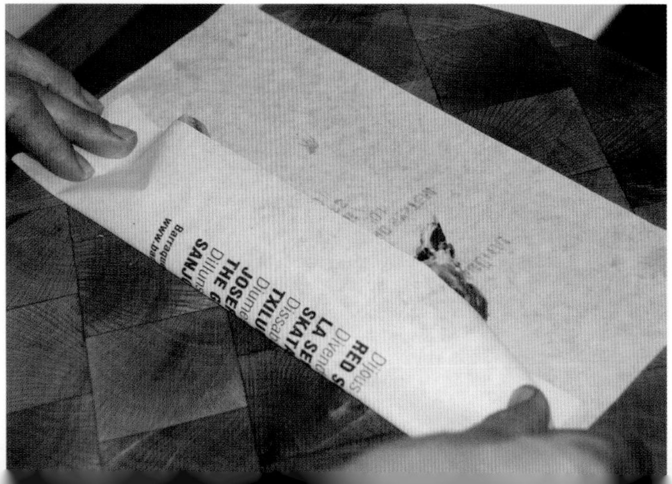

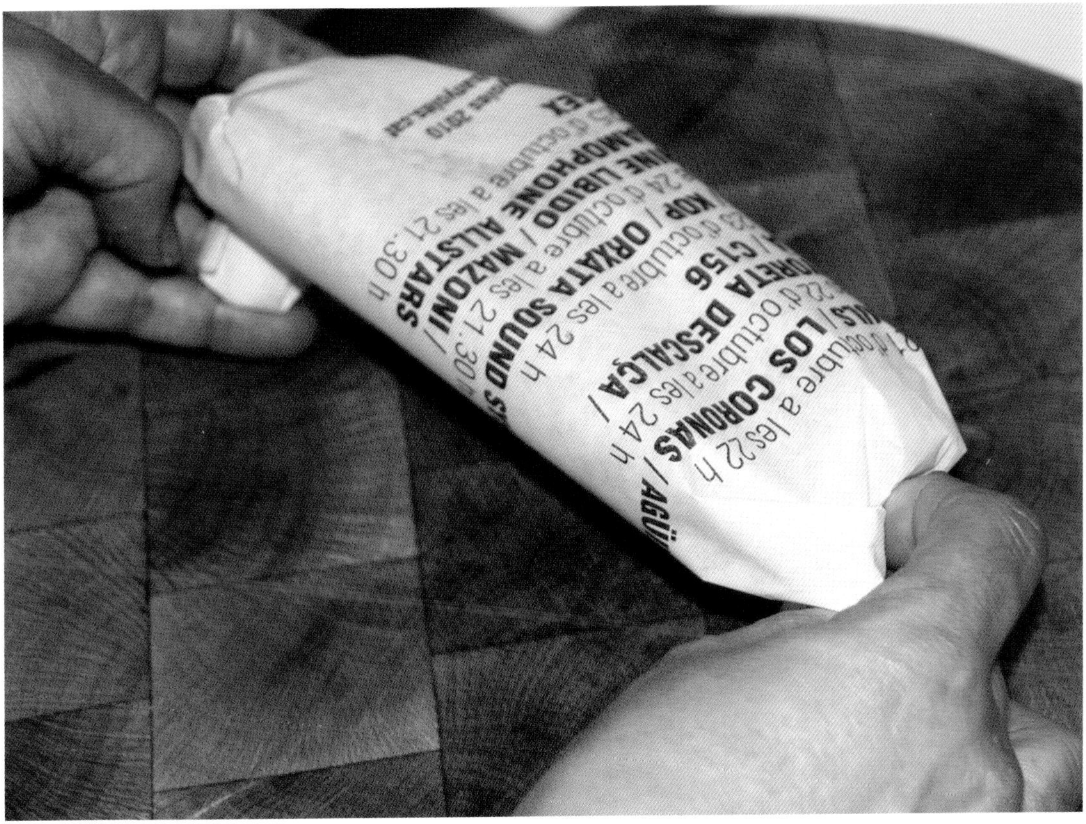

018/
Anna Pigem • *Wrapping paper for butchers with the program of Barraques. The logo of Barraques is a lamb.*

019/
estudio eckert+zúñiga • *Info-disc that search stores to promote the green commerce of the municipality.*

020/
Dúctil • *Campaign against sexual violence.*

021/
uauh! comunicación gráfica • *A tee-shirt design for the double-bass player Esperanza Spalding.*

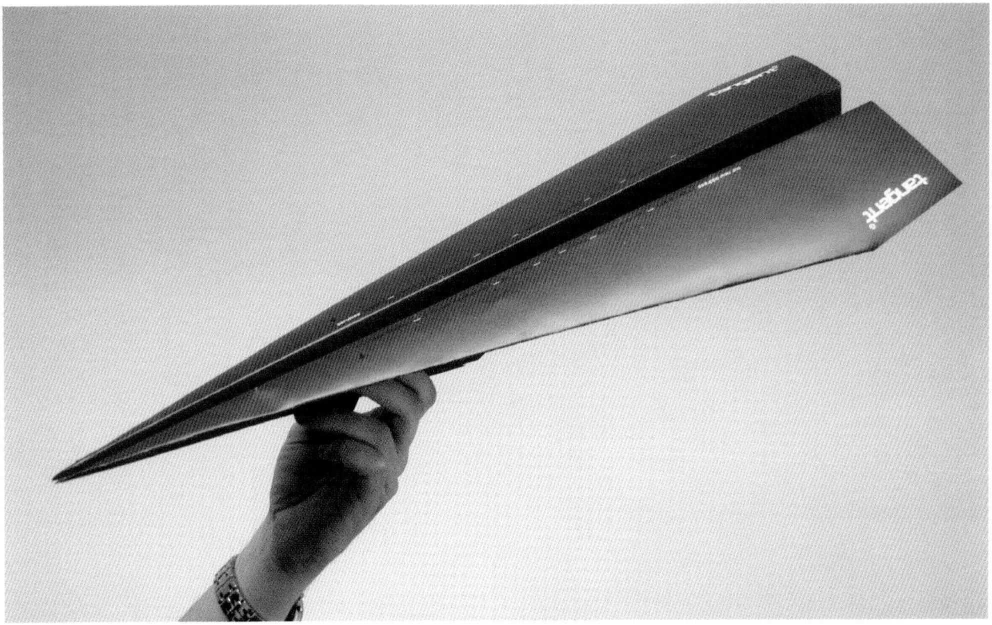

022/
Tangent Graphic • *200 A2 hand-folded planes with personalized hand written message with exact directions to our new studio in metres. Unique URL for every recipient (http://www.tangentgraphic.co.uk/aeroplane).*

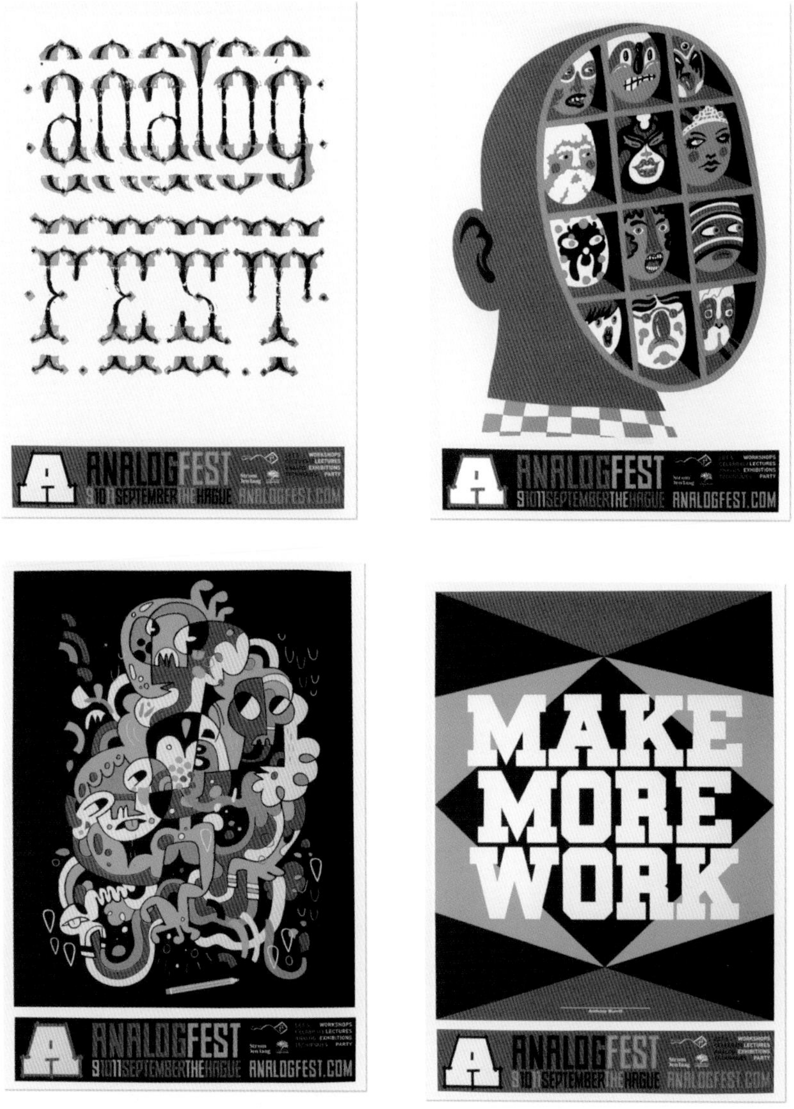

023/

Trapped in Suburbia • *'AnalogFest' is a festival that celebrates analogue techniques . We wanted to take the old techniques and bring them back to life. For the identity we've chosen to work with old Dutch wise sayings, use an old font and change it into a quirky modern version.*

ANALOGFEST
9 10 11 SEPTEMBER THE HAGUE
TECHNIQUES
LECTURES, 9 SEP • JOHN BURGERMAN (UK) • ANTHONY BURRILL (UK) • ELZA JO VAN REENEN (NL) • THEATER AAN HET SPUI • WORKSHOPS, 10 - 11 SEP
GRAFISCHE WERKPLAATS • KABK
PARTY, 11 SEP • ANALOG ATTACK! • PARTY ANALOG STYLE: DANSEN EN SJANSEN OP VETTE BEATS VAN VERSCHILLENDE INTERNATIONALE EN LOKALE TALENTEN
OLD BOYS
RAISIN BREAD
FROM THE OLD BOX
ANALOG FEST
OLD
COWS THE DITCH
BIKE
ANALOGFESTCOM
SUMPTIE
ROEST!
SN'T RUST
ANALOGFESTCOM

024/
Versátil • *Self-initated project in solidarity with the disaster in Haiti. Still life and poster.*

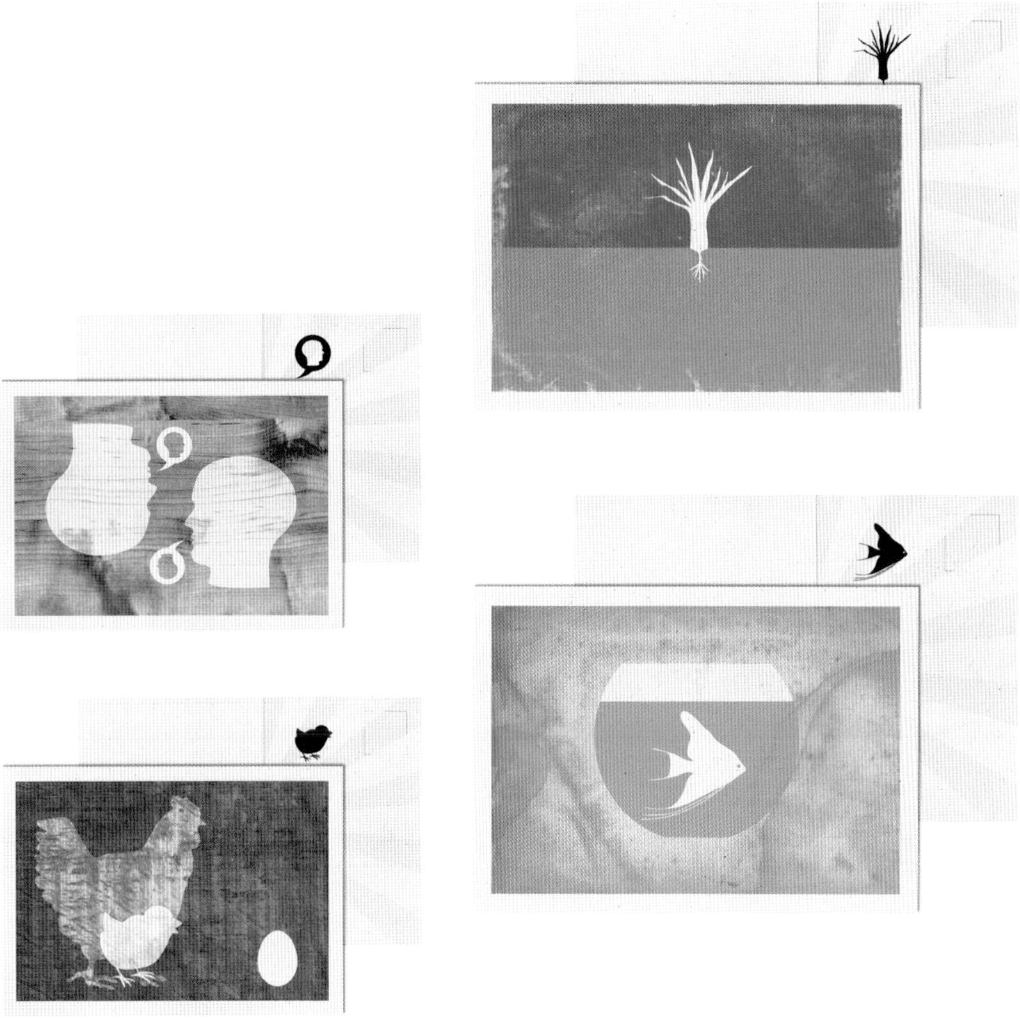

025/
EP designworks • *Postcards with handwritten notes discussing relocation.*

026/
Esther Barniol / Projectes Creatius • *To entertain, give recipes, etc., to children when they go to the restaurant with their parents.*

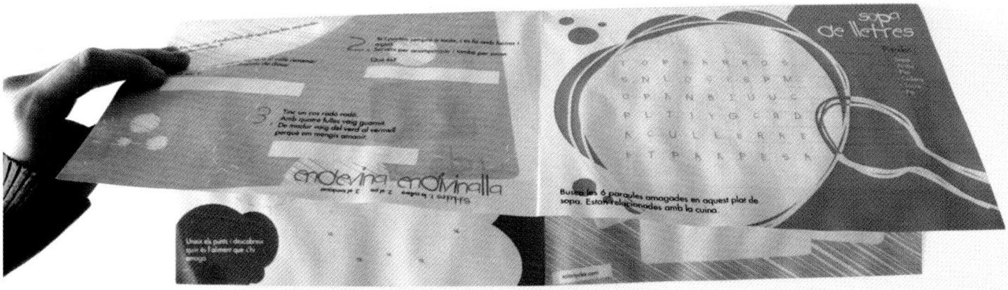
sopa de lletres
endevina endevinalla
Busca les 6 paraules amagades en aquest plat de sopa. Estan relacionades amb la cuina.

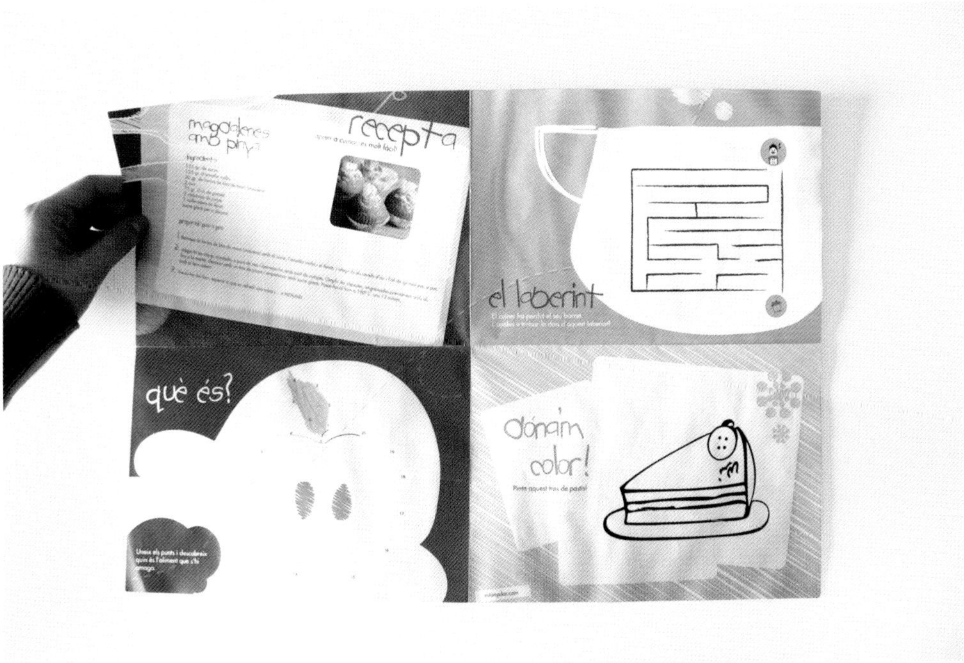
recepta
el laberint
què és?
dóna'm color!

027/
ATIPUS • *Table calendars presented as color catalogue.*

Pel juliol
beure, suar
i la fresca buscar

HOLIDAY
POP-UP SHOP!
and BENEFIT FOR REASON TO GIVE
FRIDAY DECEMBER 4 5-10PM
50% of all sales will be donated to Reason to Give families for holiday gifts.
+
50 UNDER $50 ART WALL
Featuring the work of The Firebelly Family, Art School Girl, Good Night TV, Rick Valicenti, The Post Family, Sighn, Delicious Design League, Owly Shadow Puppets and many more artist friends and generally cool people we enjoy rubbing elbows with from time to time.
at FIREBELLY DESIGN'S STUDIO: 2701 WEST THOMAS, 2ND FLOOR
in HUMBOLDT PARK. MORE INFO AT: WWW.FIREBELLYDESIGN.COM

028/
Firebelly Design • *Postcard promoted an in-studio shop that featured some of Chicago's brightest craft artisans. Proceeds benefitted Firebelly Design's non-profit, 'Reason to Give'.*

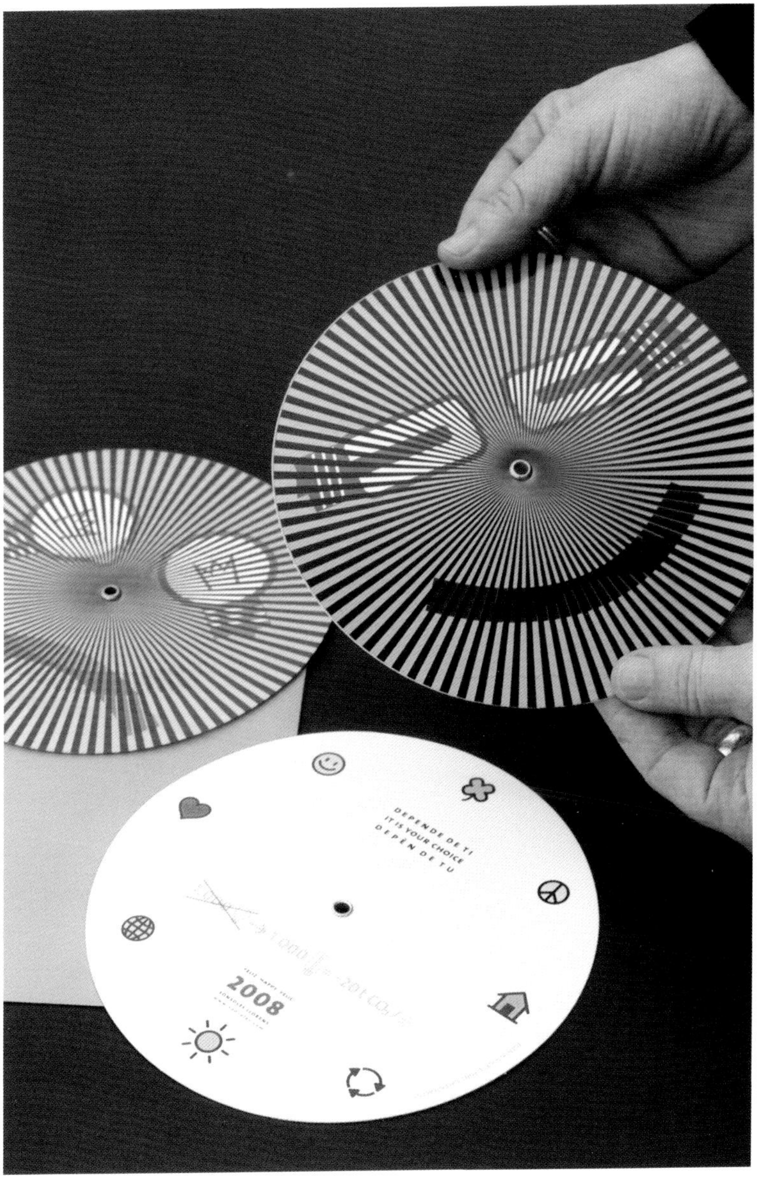

029/
Sonsoles Llorens • *An optical game to convince the necessity to use lightbulbs in an amusing way.*

Re-Bag
5-11/10/07
SEA Gallery
Airside
BB/Saunders
Browns
Design Project
MadeThought
Multistorey
NB: Studio
Non-Format
ODD
Saturday
SEA
Spin
Supermundane
The Designers Republic
Winkreative
Curated by Progress Packaging, Re-Bag is an exhibition of limited edition reusable canvas bags designed by 15 leading UK design practitioners.
Bags are available to purchase at the exhibition or from progresspkg.co.uk/re-bag or blanka.co.uk

030/
Progress Packaging • *Promotional bag for 'ReBag' show promoting reusable tote bags formats with designs by 15 leading UK practitioners in the design industry.*

031/
UVE Diseño y Comunicación, S.L. • *Corporate e-mail campaign to communicate the change of the studio's schedule to its clients and suppliers.*

Pues yo me veo perfecta.

Arial

---

brunobaeza.com

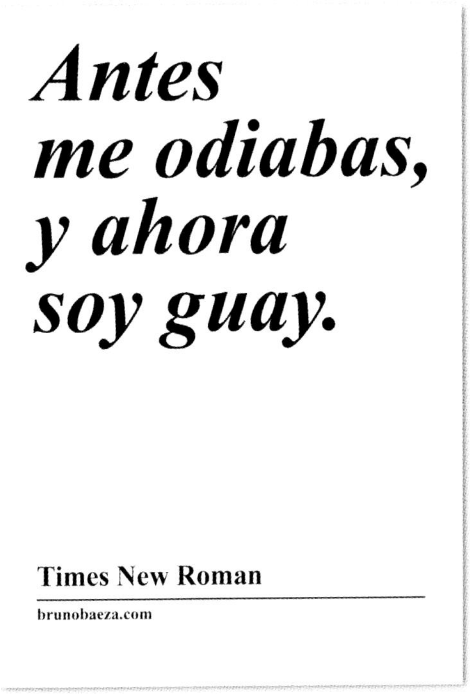
Antes
me odiabas,
y ahora
soy guay.
Times New Roman
brunobaeza.com

¡No soy
ningún
chiste!
Comic Sans
brunobaeza.com

032/
Bruno Baeza • *Post-cards addressed to designers. Well-known fonts think about themselves and their relationships with designers.*

033/
ESIETE • *Leaflet for women's clothing sales.*

Vestit
Tara Jarmon
Clutch
Som-Mits
Sabates
Paco Herrero
Ulleres
Spitfire
Biquini
Bluegirl

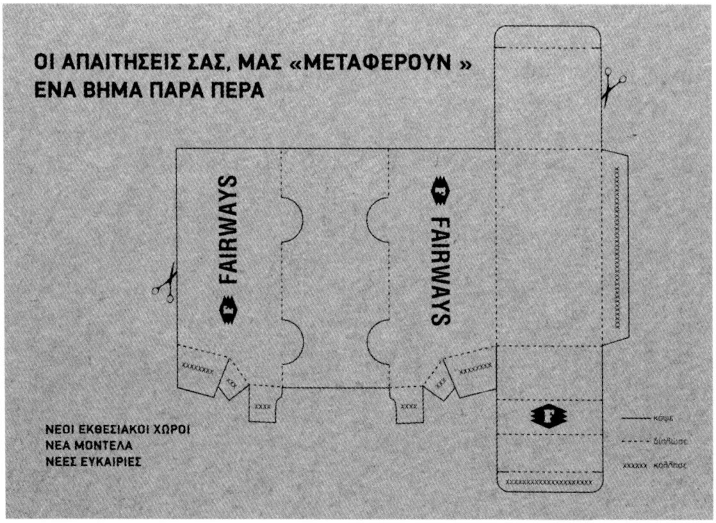

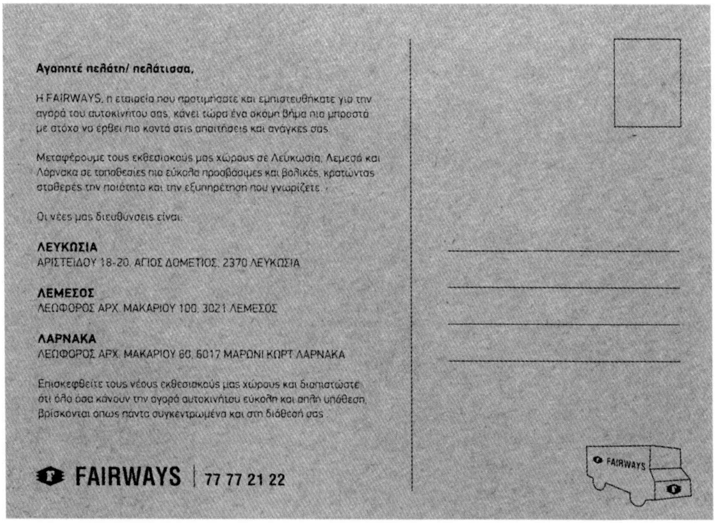

034/
Design By Alpha • *Direct mail to inform clients that Fairways are moving all their car showrooms.*

ΟΙ ΑΠΑΙΤΗΣΕΙΣ ΣΑΣ ΜΑΣ «ΜΕΤΑΦΕΡΟΥΝ »
ΕΝΑ ΒΗΜΑ ΠΑΡΑ ΠΕΡΑ
FAIRWAYS
FAIRWAYS
FAIRWAYS
ΝΕΟΙ ΕΚΘΕΣΙΑΚΟΙ ΧΩΡΟΙ
ΝΕΑ ΜΟΝΤΕΛΑ
ΝΕΕΣ ΕΥΚΑΙΡΙΕΣ

ΟΙ ΑΠΑΙΤΗΣΕΙΣ ΣΑΣ ΜΑΣ
ΕΝΑ ΒΗΜΑ ΠΑΡΑ ΠΕΡΑ
FAIRWAYS
ΝΕΟΙ ΕΚΘΕΣΙΑΚΟΙ ΧΩΡΟΙ
ΝΕΑ ΜΟΝΤΕΛΑ
ΝΕΕΣ ΕΥΚΑΙΡΙΕΣ

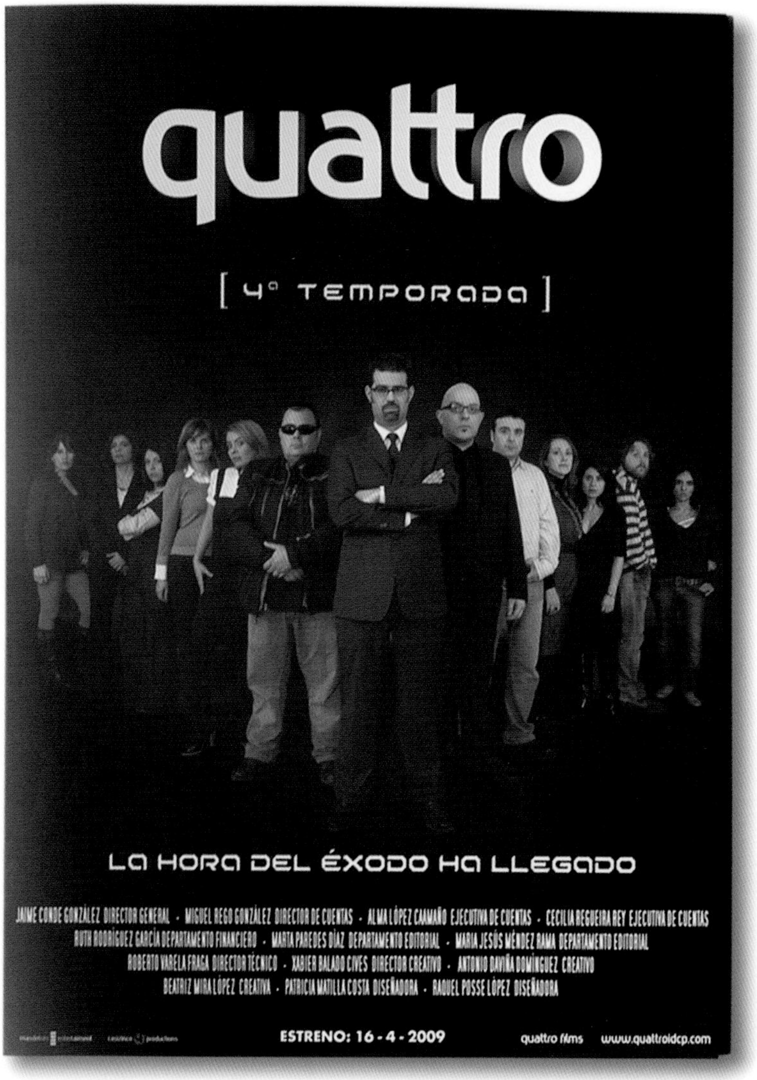

035/
Quattro idcp • *Communication from the Quattro idcp to clients and suppliers to inform them that the head office has changed, using a press book inspired by a fictional TV series.*

quattro
invitación
quattro
sinopsis
quattro

quattro
quattro

001/ - Promo number
Albertini Romain - Studio name
Club Blister - Client name
France - Country

CLUB BLISTER is a London- and Paris-based collective of DJs, designers, musicians and promoters. - Promo description

001/
Albertini Romain
Club Blister
France

CLUB BLISTER is a London- and Paris-based collective of DJs, designers, musicians and promoters.

002/
Claudia Dionne/Ibo Angulo
Perro de Mundo
Mexico

Handmade press kit: The idea is for the style, creativity and inspirations linked to the concept to jump out to its readers.

003/
Trapped in Suburbia
Self-initiated
The Netherlands

We wanted to get our clients moving behind their desks, so we created this notebook with writing space on one side and patterns from different balls on the other. Just attach a piece of paper to a ball and you can play soccer or rugby, or you can throw a tennis ball in your waste basket.

004/
Foreign Policy Design Group
Self-promotion
Singapore

Calendar/Announcement card.
Card Creative Direction/Art Direction: Yah-Leng Yu, Arthur Chin.
Design: Tianyu Isaiah Zheng (TY).
Copy: Arthur Chin.

005/
Pepe Gimeno - Proyecto Gráfico
OTH
Spain

In order to promote and disclose how they work, the Habitat Tendencies' Observer provides training materials such as 'WAKE UP!'.

006/
Flou Flou - disoñadores asociados
Personal project
Spain

2008 materials for 'Disechos', an annual meeting that allows for temporary spaces of dialogue, reflection and work, using creative and technical disciplines.

007/
MadeThought
Design Miami
United Kingdom

Promotional bag for 'Design Miami Basel' show.

008/
la regadera grafica | Albert Terré
Agramunt Town
Spain

To promote the nougat and pure melting chocolate festival with aprons.

009/
ATIPUS
Self-promotion
Spain

To announce to the clients the days that the studio will be closed for the holidays ATIPUS has created some illustrations that evoke summer travels.

010/
Sublima Comunicación
Sublima Comunicación
Spain

Self-promotional calendar on fabric with buttons to point out dates.

011/
Raúl Iglesias Design
Self-promotion
Spain

Promotional poster mailed to studios and potential clients. It plays on the phrase 'Use me to relax' and is covered in bubble wrap. It contains a shortened version of my CV, including relevant information and a selection of some of my projects.

012/
Bunch
The Star of Bethnal Green
Croatia

The project evolved from Bunch being chosen to devise a distinct identity for The Star of Bethnal Green in 2008. A traditional long-tailed star was taken and illustrated to create artwork that represented the corresponding month. This was applied each month for approximately a year with all of the illustration done in house by Bunch.

013/
&Larry
General Insurance Association
Singapore

This calendar was produced for the participants of the Talent Outreach Project. As a year-end promotional gift, it serves dual functions: one side acts a calendar, and the other side pays tribute to contributors for their year-long support.

014/
Kanella
Kanella
Greece

Happy and Sweet. A set of 12 chocolates inspired by the corresponding12 months of the year. It works as a calendar…
and each chocolate has to be eaten at the end of the corrisponding month.

015/
Jorge Lorenzo Diseño y Comunicación Visual S.L.
Self-promotion
Spain

Self-promotional calendar.

016/
Esther Barniol / Projectes Creatius
Restaurant Estany Clar
Spain

Each time a dish is brought to the table, the server also provides the name of the dish on a die-cut circle. At the end of the meal, the customer may take all the circles to remember what he or she ate. Photos: David Barra.

017/
Toben
Self-promotion
Australia

Limited edition calendar that was produced for Toben's launch in January 2010.

018/
Anna Pigem
Agrupació de Barraques
Cyprus

Wrapping paper for butchers with the program of Barraques. The logo of Barraques is a lamb.
Photos: Andrea Leria.

019/
estudio eckert+zúñiga
Sant Pol de Mar Town
Spain

Info-disc that search stores to promote the green commerce of the municipality.

020/
Dúctil
Personal project
Spain

Campaign against sexual violence.

021/
uauh! comunicación gráfica
Montuno Producciones
Spain

A tee-shirt design for the double-bass player Esperanza Spalding.

022/
Tangent Graphic
Self-promotion
United Kingdom

200 A2 hand-folded planes with personalized hand written message with exact directions to our new studio in metres. Unique URL for every recipient (http://www.tangentgraphic.co.uk/aeroplane).

023/
Trapped in Suburbia
Self-promotion
The Netherlands

'AnalogFest' is a festival that celebrates analogue techniques . We wanted to take the old techniques and bring them back to life. For the identity we've chosen to work with old Dutch wise sayings, use an old font and change it into a quirky modern version.

024/
Versátil
El Beso Producciones
Spain

Self-initated project in solidarity with the disaster in Haiti. Still life and poster.

025/
EP designworks
Self-promotion
United States

Postcards with handwritten notes discussing relocation.

026/
Esther Barniol / Projectes Creatius
Restaurant Estany Clar
Spain

To entertain, give recipes, etc., to children when they go to the restaurant with their parents.

027/
ATIPUS
Self-promotion
Spain

Table calendars presented as color catalogue.

028/
Firebelly Design
Reason to Give
United States

Postcard promoted an in-studio shop that featured some of Chicago's brightest craft artisans. Proceeds benefitted Firebelly Design's non-profit, 'Reason to Give'.

029/
Sonsoles Llorens
Personal project
Spain

An optical game to convince the necessity to use lightbulbs in an amusing way.

030/
Progress Packaging
Progress Packaging
United Kingdom

Promotional bag for 'ReBag' show promoting reusable tote bags formats with designs by 15 leading UK practitioners in the design industry.

031/
UVE Diseño y Comunicación, S.L.
Self-promotion
Spain

Corporate e-mail campaign to communicate the change of the studio's schedule to its clients and suppliers.

032/
Bruno Baeza
Self-promotion
Spain

Post-cards addressed to designers. Well-known fonts think about themselves and their relationships with designers.

033/
ESIETE
Les Orenetes
Spain

Leaflet for women's clothing sales.

034/
Design By Alpha
Fairways Motor
Cyprus

Direct mail to inform clients that Fairways are moving all their car showrooms.

035/
Quattro idcp
Self-promotion
Spain

Communication from the Quattro idcp to clients and suppliers to inform them that the head office has changed,using a press book inspired by a fictional TV series.

To Celebrate
070 - 147

036/
ZORRAQUINO • *A small carton box-Christmas gift, filled with 12 teabags of digestive infusions related to the 12 days of the 'Advent calendar'. Each 'Happy digestion' teabag was prescribed to be enjoyed after the abundant holiday meals of the season (e.g., Christmas Eve dinner, company's Christmas lunch, etc.).*

037/
Gorka Aizpurua Serrano • *Christmas greetings leaflet sent with a magnifying glass, because small details are very often the most important.*

038/
Zigurat Comunicación Gráfica, S.L. • *Our best wishes with a message in a five-panel leaflet that we send to our clients and friends.*

PALABR
zigurat Comunicación
Sinceramente...
new web
check it
next 15.1.09
www.ziguratcomunicacion.es
don pedro, 6. 1°ext. 28005 madrid

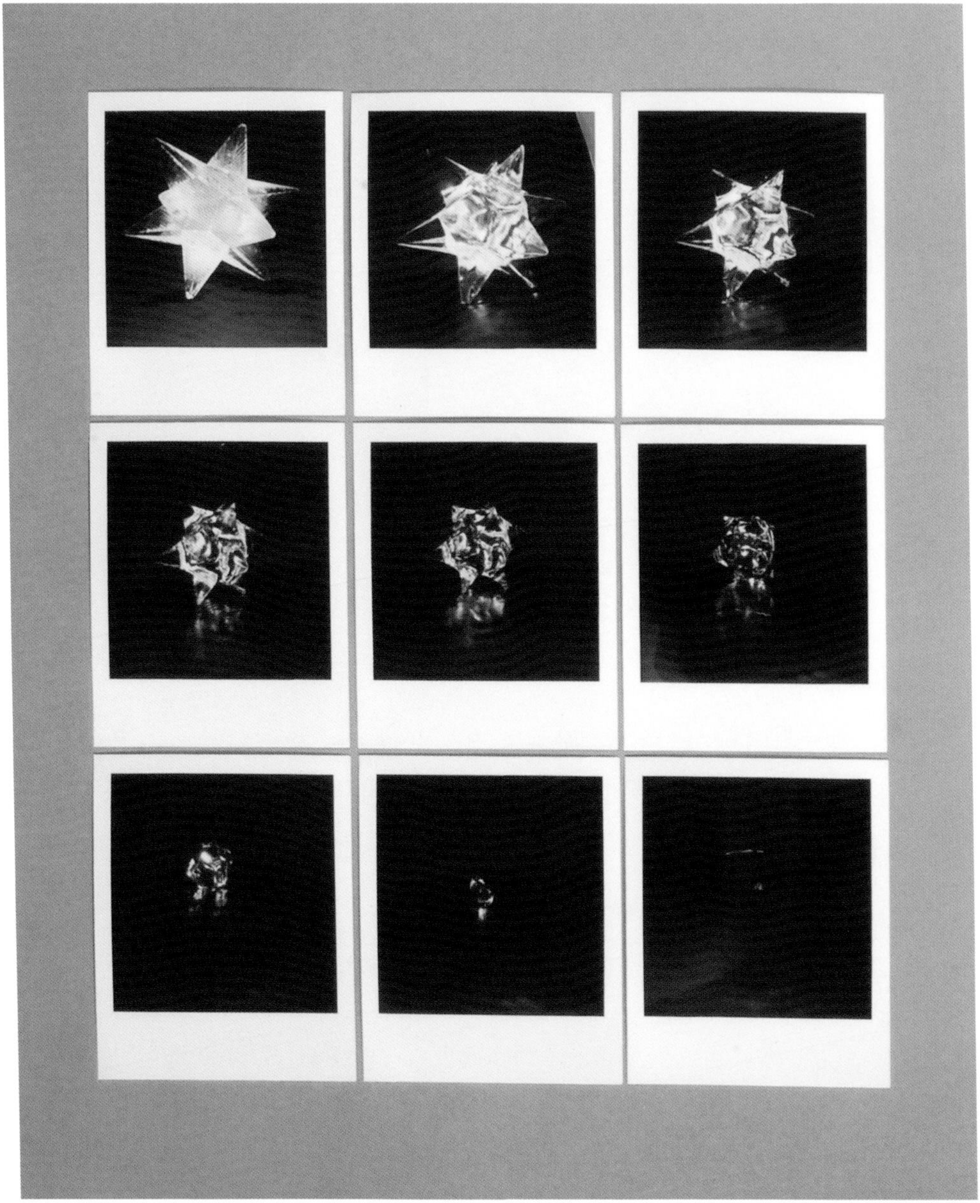

039/

KentLyons • *For our 2009 Christmas card, a 50 cm² 12-pointed Moravian star, hand-carved from ice, was left to melt over 15 hours. We documented this process with Polaroid film and sent the results out as cards to our friends.*

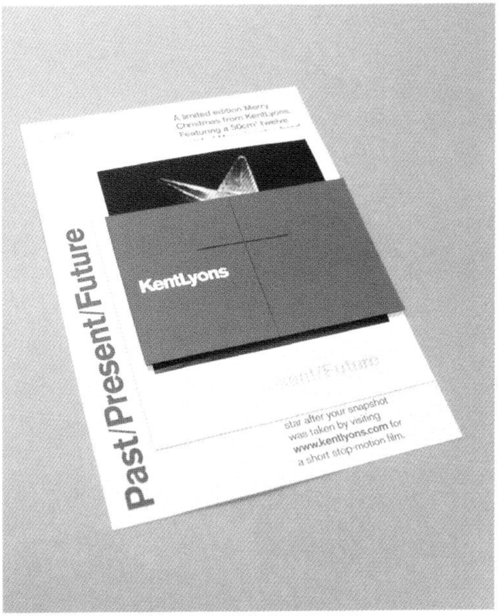
A limited edition Merry
Christmas from KentLyons.
Featuring a 50cm³ twelve
Past/Present/Future
KentLyons
star after your snapshot
was taken by visiting
www.kentlyons.com for
a short stop-motion film.

KentLyons

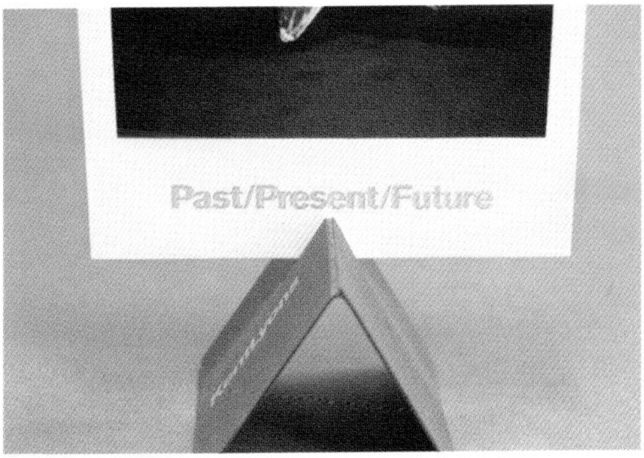
Past/Present/Future

040/

Lucía Castro • *The Majoral's Christmas postcard shows the Fiji collection wrapped in vine leaves. The representation and the enclosure try to convey this concept.*

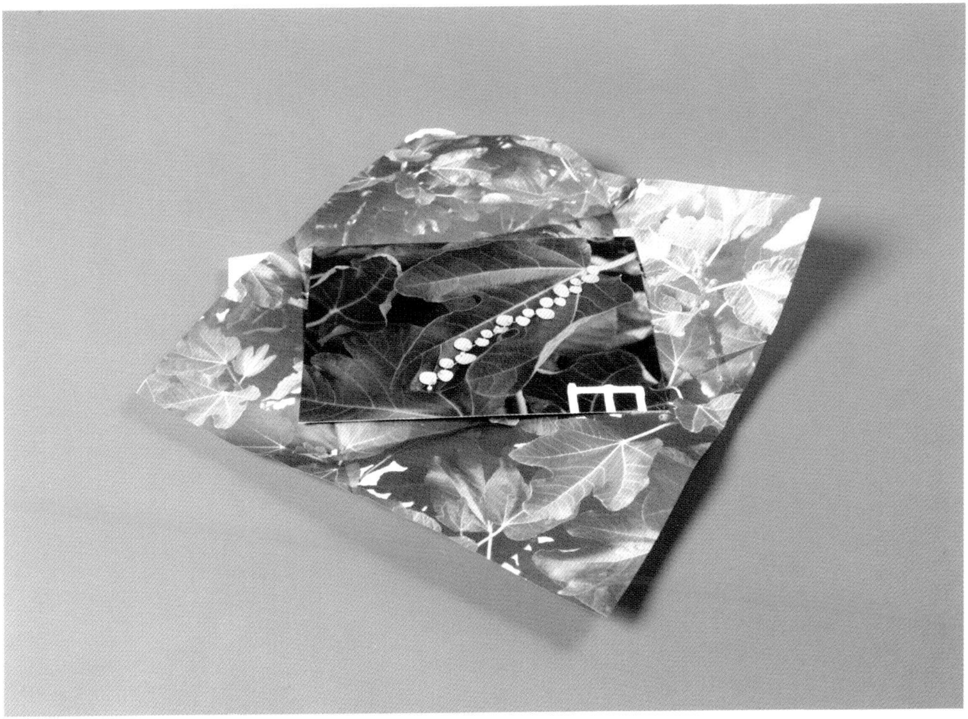

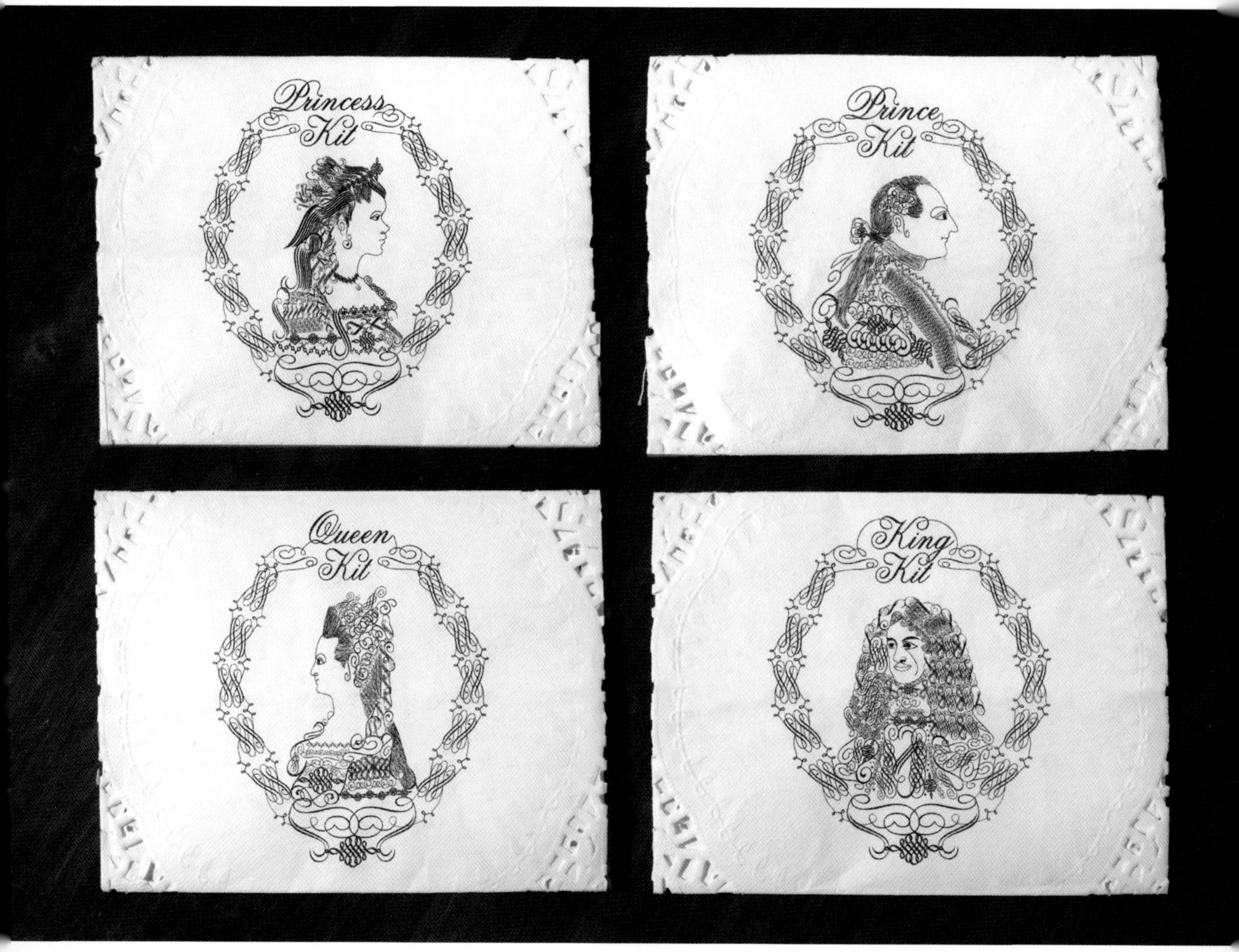

041/

Carlitos y Patricia | Idea Boutique • *More than a simple gift-card, the gift-kits from the 5°1ª Beauty Salon are a present themselves. Besides a personalized beauty treatment, each kit contains a surprise-object: a frog for the Princess kit, a blue paint pastille for the Prince kit and a Swedish crown for the King and Queen kits. Hand-made and printed with a laser printer from low-cost standard material.*

5º 1ª
Prince Kit
Princess Kit
Queen Kit
King Kit

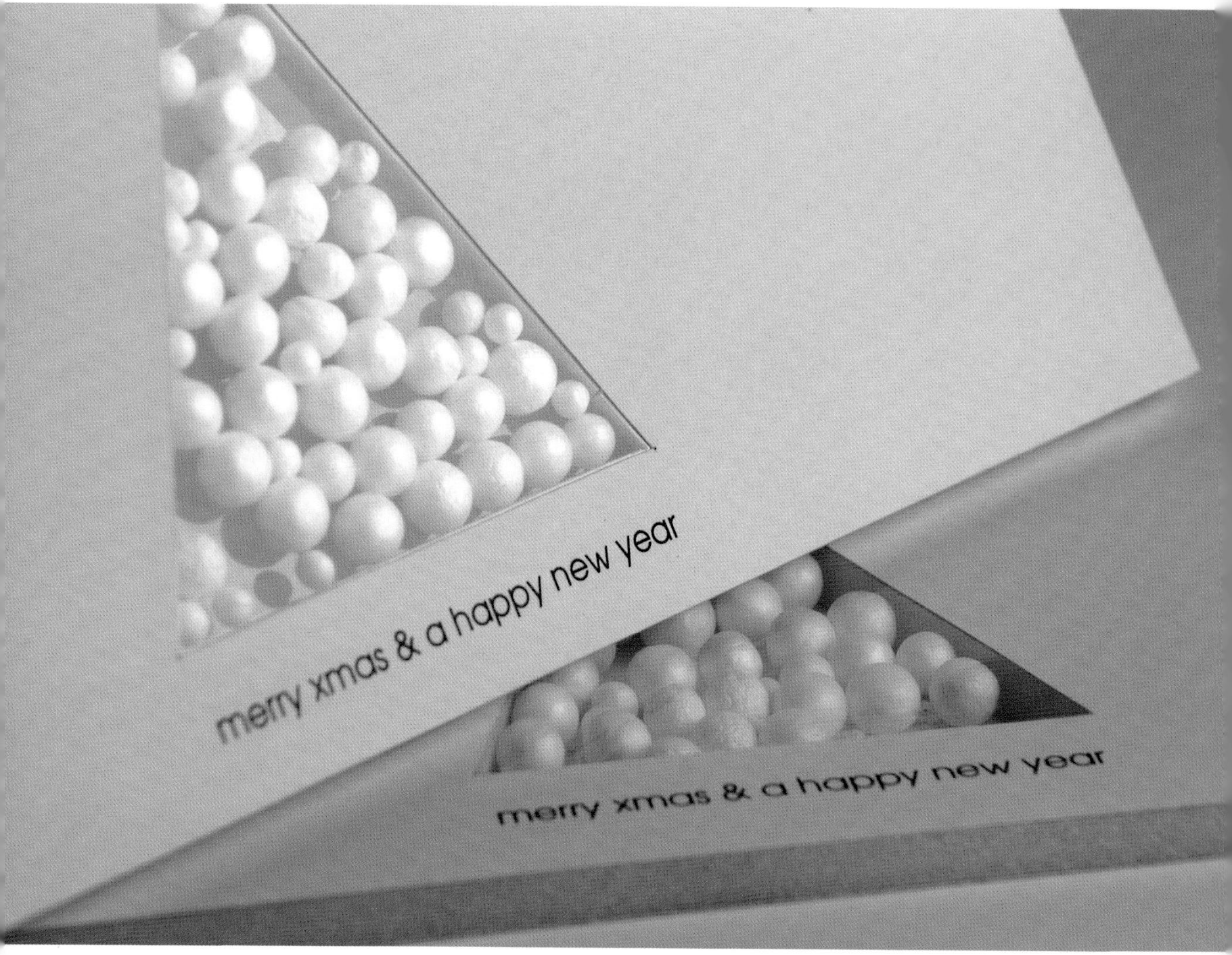
merry xmas & a happy new year
merry xmas & a happy new year

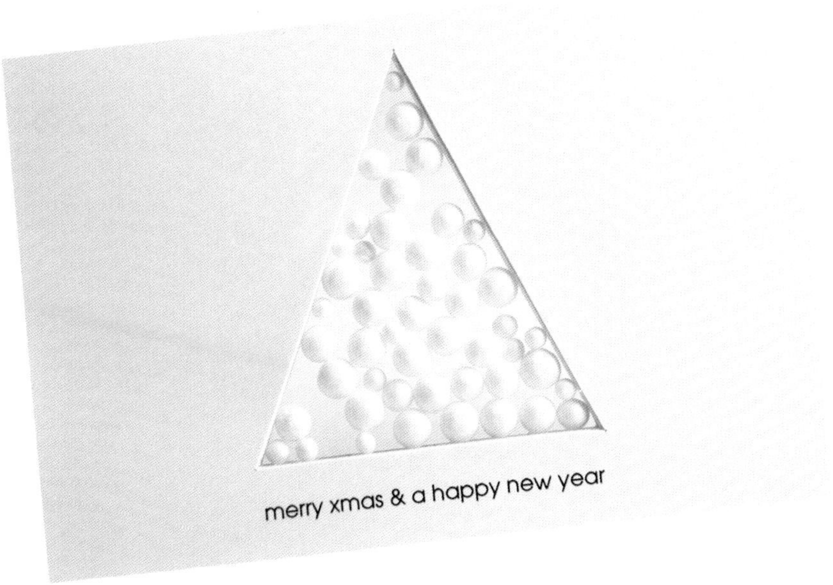

042/
take off - media services • *Development of a promotional tool for our design agency: an extraordinary Christmas mailing filled with polystyrene balls.*

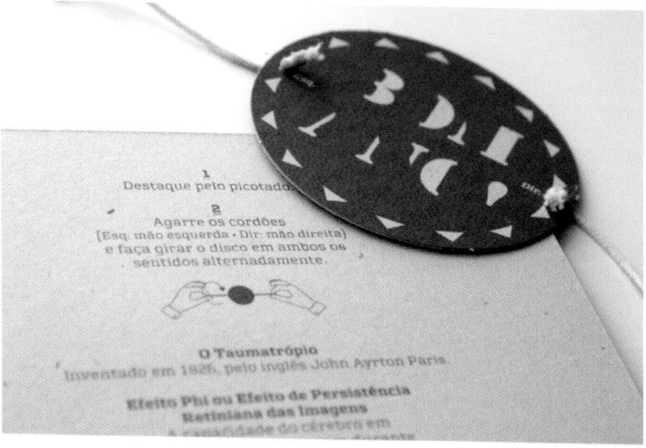

043/

Flatland Design • *Card sent to Flatland's clients, partners and friends with a New Year's message. Original and playful solution was used to decipher the message, encouraging interaction with the object. The 2010 New Year's card includes a thaumatrope.*

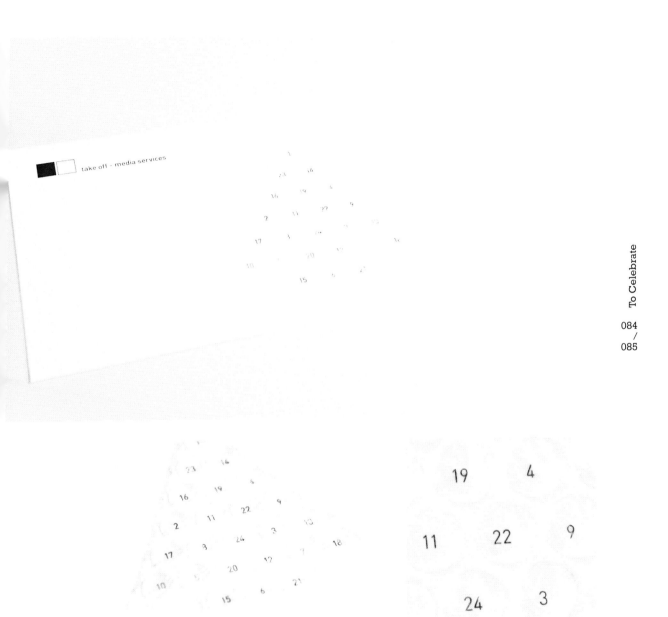

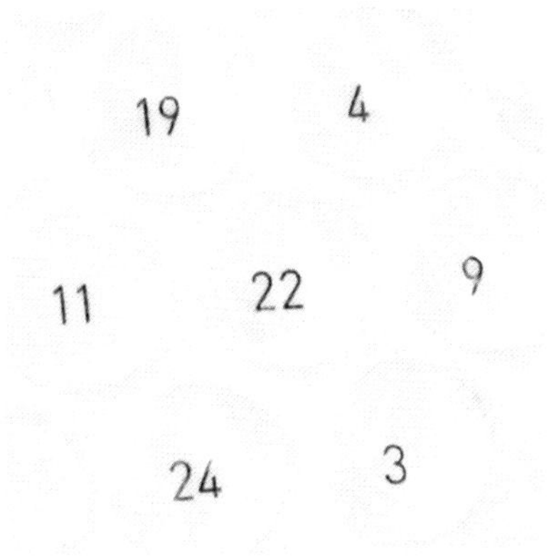

044/
take off - media services • *Development of a promotion-tool for our design agency: an extraordinary Christmasmailing in form of an advent calendar.*

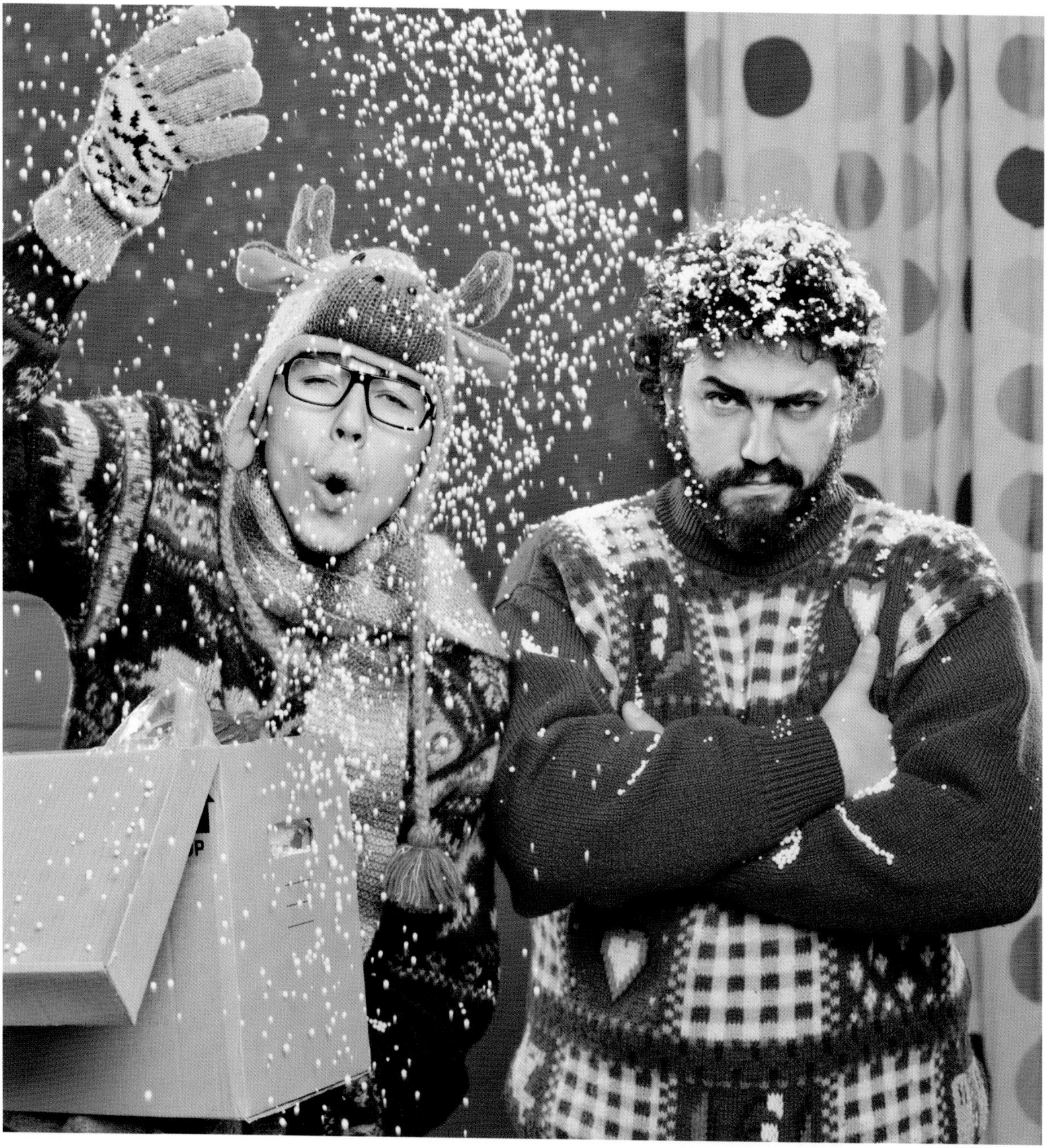

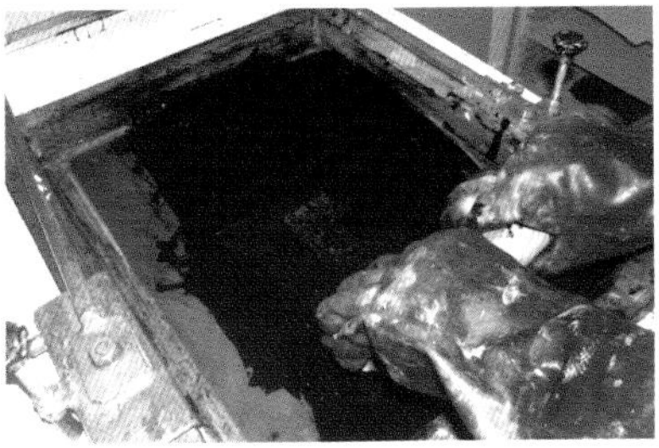

045/
SOPA Graphics • *Christmas greetings. A package of false snow for real people.*

MUJI NOEL MACHINE
無印良品サンタ販売機
MUJI

046/
Carlitos y Patricia | Idea Boutique • *What would Santa Claus look like if he were Japanese? He'd be a vending machine. From this idea we built the MUJI Noel Machine, a vending machine to attract customers to the Spanish MUJI stores. The shops were crowded and the action generated buzz in more than 40 countries.*

El día 19 vas a
brindar en colores

9.000
DÍAS DE COLOR
9.000
DÍAS DE COLOR

047/
El Cuartel • *Artigraf printers from Malaga celebrated their 25th anniversary. A mailing invitation with three messages.*

encuentra nuestros mejores
deseos entre la nieve
¿otra
navidad
sin nieve?
Muy lejos te tendrás que ir estas navidades
si quieres pasarlas sobre un manto blanco.

048/

Sublima Comunicación • *As the saying goes: 'Snowy year, good year'. Taking into consideration that this enterprise has almost all the clients in Murcia, where it never snows, cork snow was sent to them to wish prosperity during the year.*

049/
Flatland Design • *Card sent to Flatland's clients, partners, and friends with a New Year's message. Original and playful solution was used to decipher the message, encouraging interaction with the object. The 2009 New Year's card uses solar light.*

050/
Uniform • *An alternative to the usual Christmas card, we created a foil-stamped, typographical 'Closed' sign for clients to hang on their doors as they close shop for the holidays.*

OPEN
Please deliver to:
OPEN
Please deliver to:

Sorry
We are closed for the holidays
* For
Mulled wine and mince pies, wrapping presents,

051/
Vertigo Graphix • *We offer to clients and friends a piece to greet them for Christmas and to give them lots of positive energy in these financially difficult times. A wink to surprise them.*

052/
Maddison Graphic • *We designed this card to wish our friends and clients a happy Christmas and also to announce our new Website. It is foil blocked black and white on heavy grey board.*

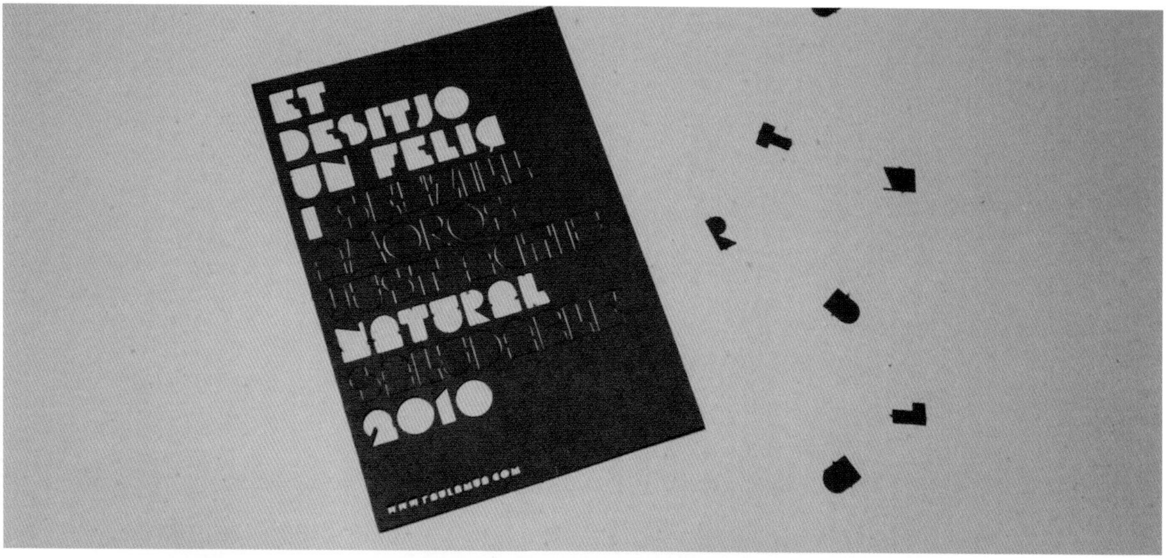

053/
Vellut • *Promotional postcard to greet the New Year. The user can choose the wish that he or she prefers and complete the piece after reading the usual 'Happy New Year 2010'.*

054/
Aloof • *Christmas card and promotion for the salon's luxury hairdressing service, 'Realhair Privé'.*

055/
Pepe Gimeno - Proyecto Gráfico • *A graphic intervention to create a Christmas'-like atmosphere with cardboard trees in different scales.*

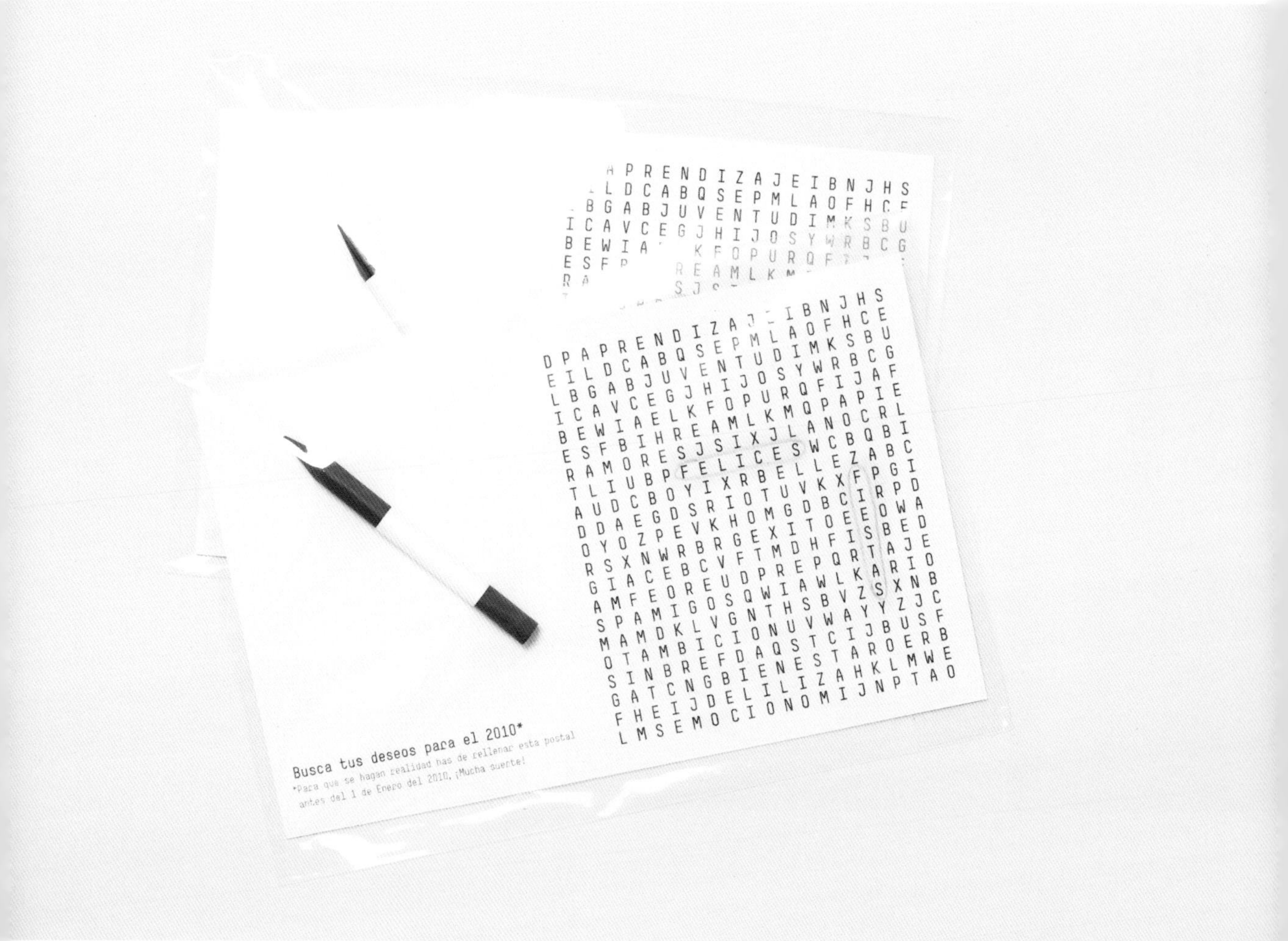
Busca tus deseos para el 2010*
*Para que se hagan realidad has de rellenar esta postal antes del 1 de Enero del 2010. ¡Mucha suerte!

056/
Lucía Castro • *Go for your wishes in 2010. By completing this a crossword puzzle you find the wishes that you want to fulfil for your new year, such as: happiness, learning, love...*

Busca tus deseos para el 2010*

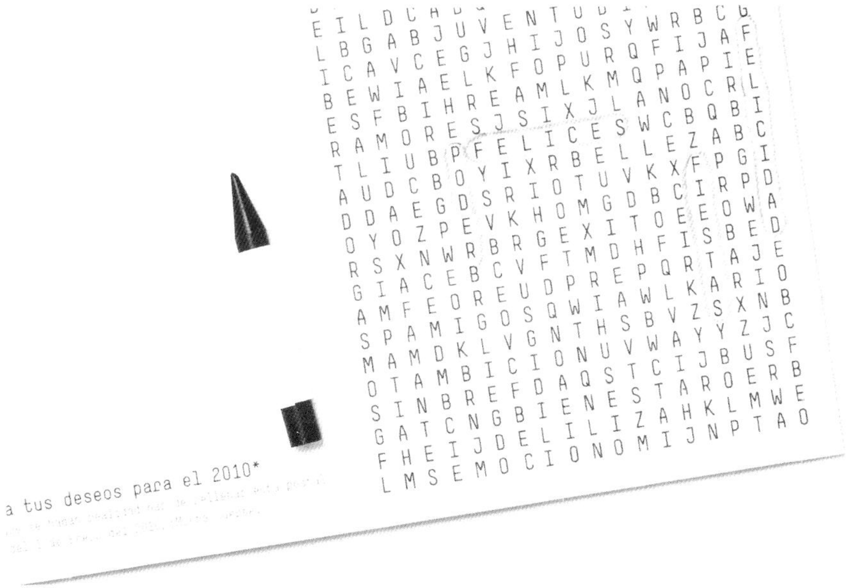
a tus deseos para el 2010*

BON
NADAL I
FELIÇ ANY
NOU

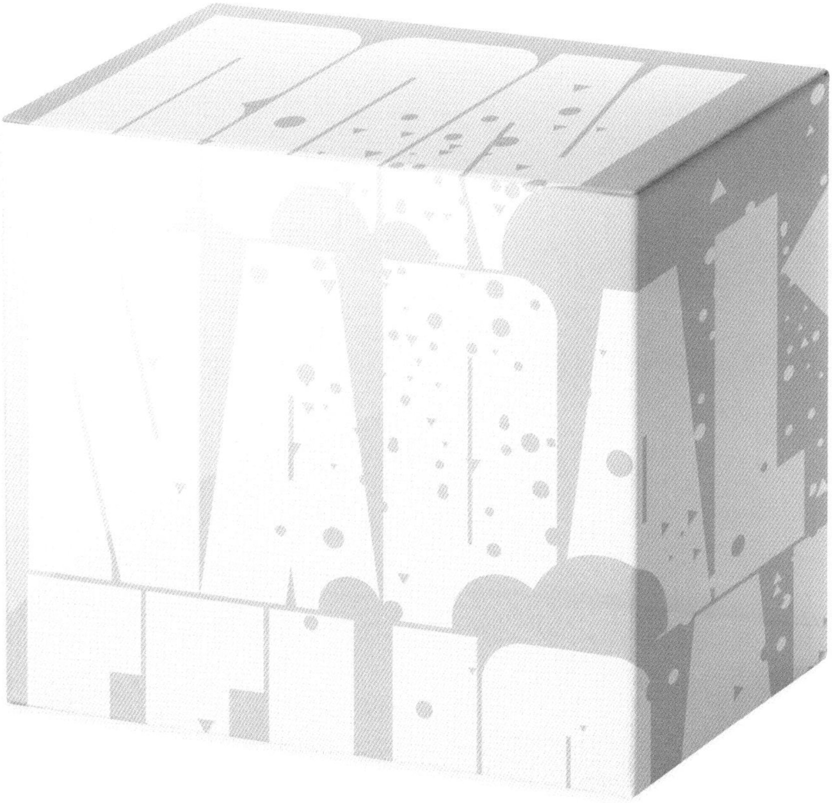

057/
TwoPoints.Net • *TwoPoints.Net has designed the New Year's greetings for the 'Col.legi Oficial Disseny Gràfic Catalunya'. Instead of sending a postcard or chocolates, we wanted to make a useful Christmas gift. And what else is more useful than wrapping paper? The font was specifically designed for this project.*

058/
The Creative Method • *The aim was to create a unique gift to give to our clients at Christmas and to act as a new business introduction. We obtained high-quality cleanskin wines and created our own labels.*

BYO
BUILD YOUR
SAINT CLAIR
BUT SERIOUSLY...
BYO
BUILD YOUR OWN Andri.
SAINT CLAIR
09 Sauvignon Blanc | Marlborough

059/
StudioCentro Marketing srl • *There are two ways to face the future: use a talisman or contact a group of professionals like the members of StudioCentro Marketing.*

060/
CUBO DISEÑO • *The most traditional Christmas greeting is a postcard. We wanted to greet our clients in this way, but with a different and very sweet touch.*

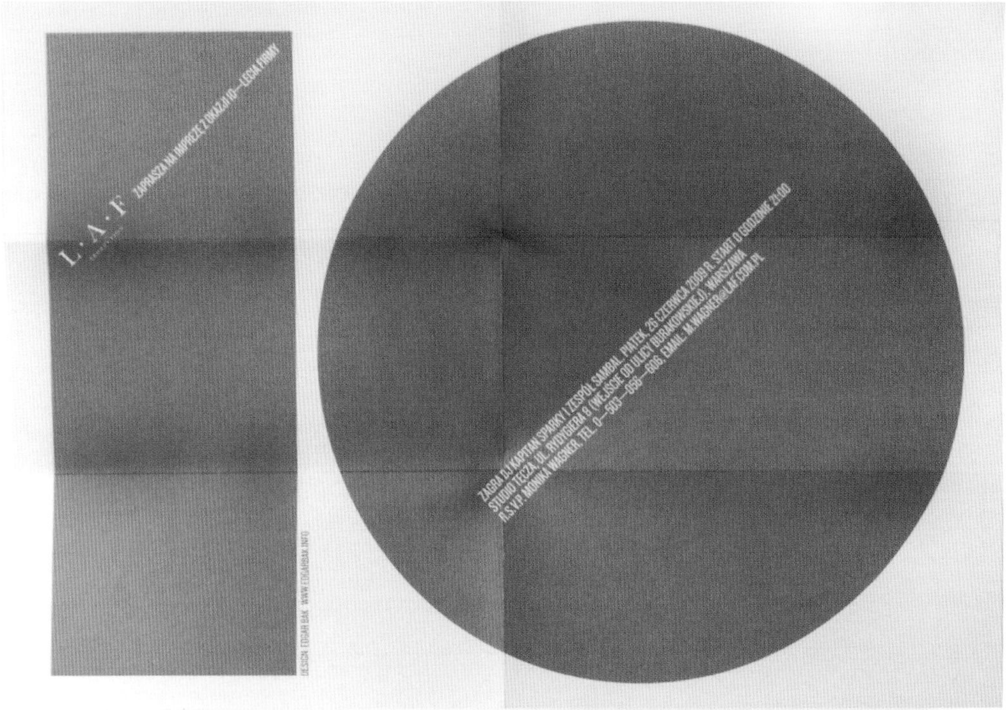

061/
Edgar Bak • *10 years' anniversary invitation. Golden pantone on offset paper.*

062/
Gorka Aizpurua Serrano • *Feliz año nueve. Promotional New Year's greeting from the author. Because of the financial crisis he prefers to donate 9 cents to his best friends, which is the cost of the making of a postcard.*

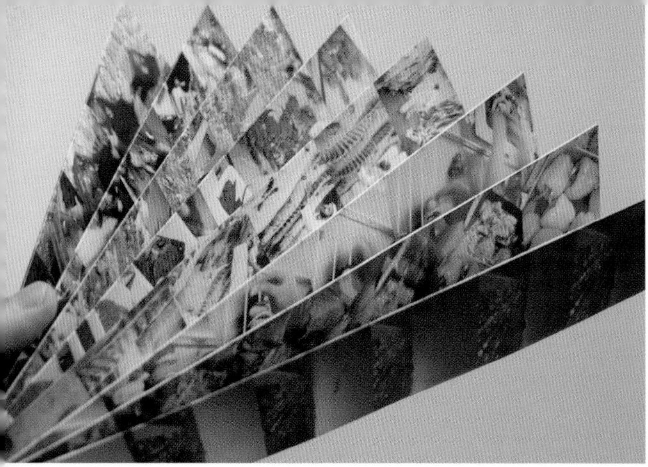

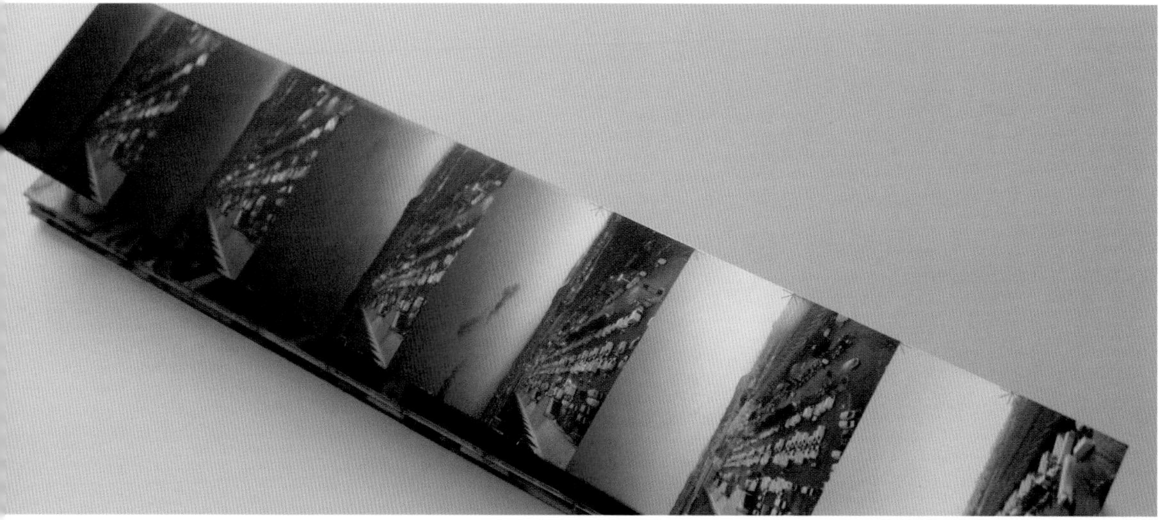

063/
extra! • *A star-shaped greeting leaflet. The idea is to wish a happy New Year showing the Mercabarna day-to-day activities, in daily sequences.*

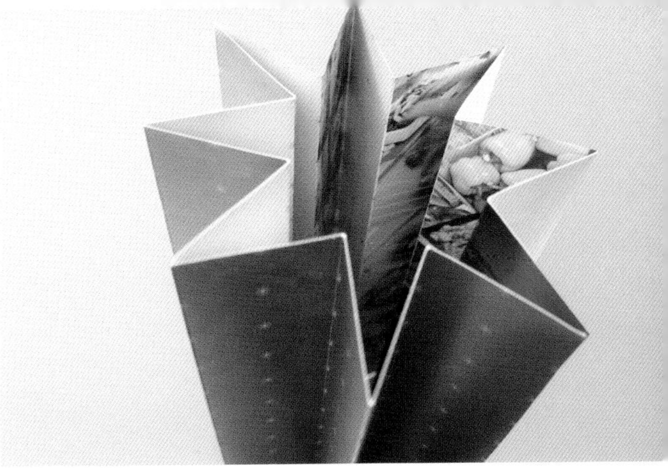

064/
Ryszard Bienert / 3group • *New Year's postcard. Brocade and gold foil stamping. Year of publication: December 2010.*

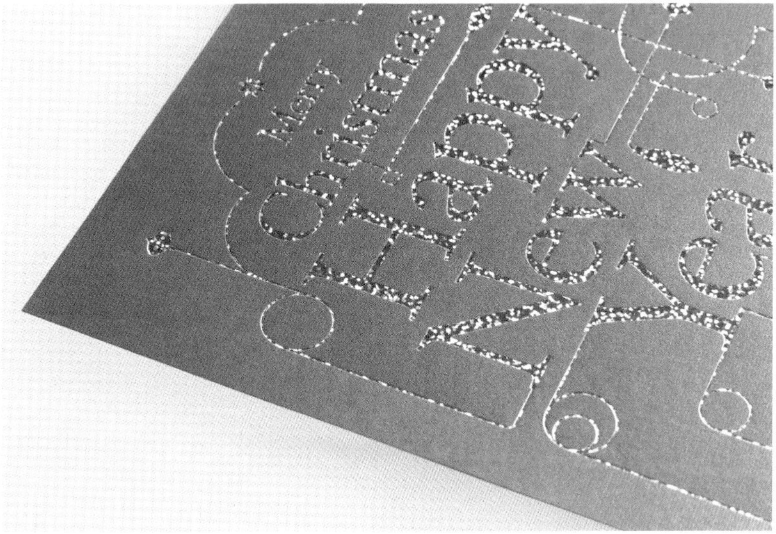
Merry
Christmas
Happy
New

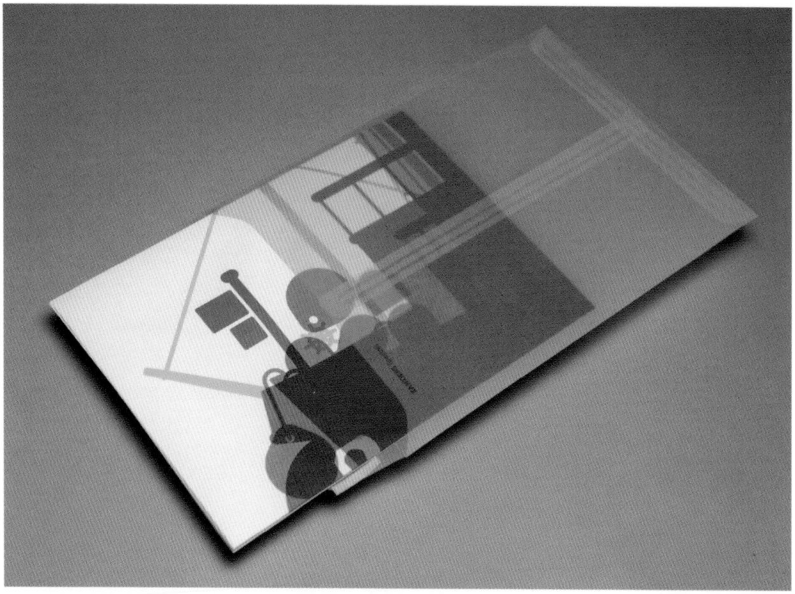

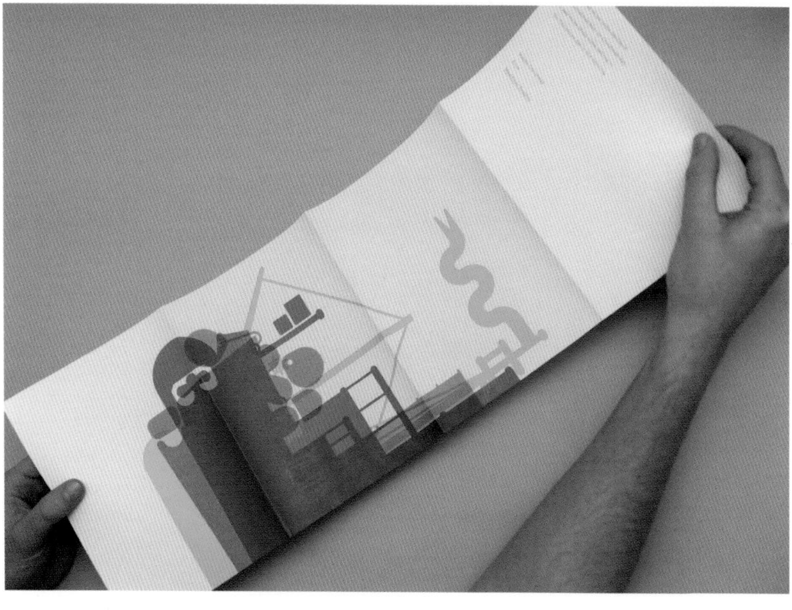

065/
Maddison Graphic • *Our Christmas card for 2010 depicts three ships overprinted on Offenbach bible paper.*

066/
Clay McIntosh Creative • *A true 'green' project that uses recycled promo items to create a pop-up Christmas card promotion.*

067/
The Creative Method • *The Creative Method were moving to a new office space, and it was also Christmas time. The idea was to show both.*

068/
Menta • *Season´s greeting card inspired by the geometric structures and surfaces projected in the architectural work of Tomas Llavador.*

JOSÉ MARÍA TOMÁS LLAVADOR
Y SU EQUIPO LES DESEAN FELICES FIESTAS
Y UN PRÓSPERO AÑO 2010

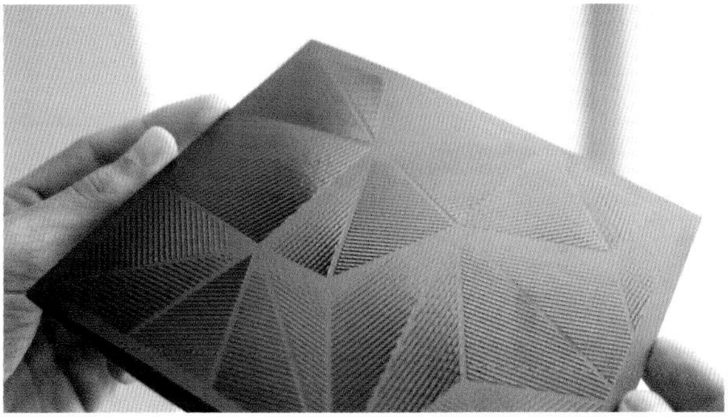

069/
Nikolaus Schmidt Design • *Season's greetings for clients and friends.*

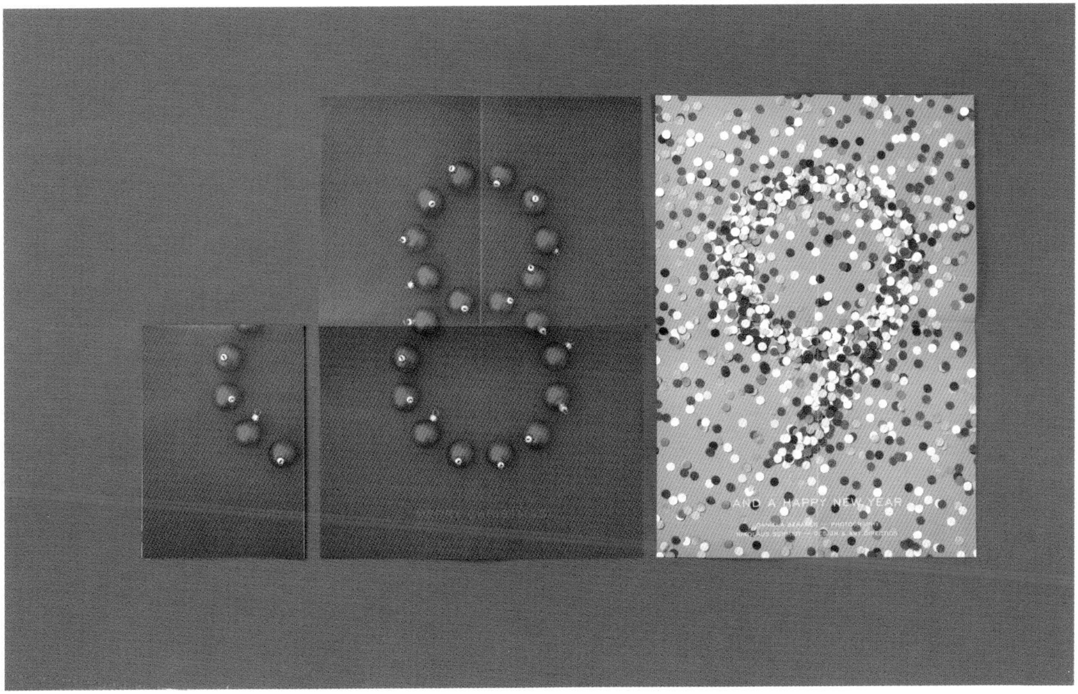
AND A HAPPY NEW YEAR

PORQUE
CINCO
AÑOS
NO SON
UN JUEGO

070/
gestocomunicación • *A direct campaign mail to promote the 5th anniversary party of gestocomunicación using the message 'Because five years are not a game'.*

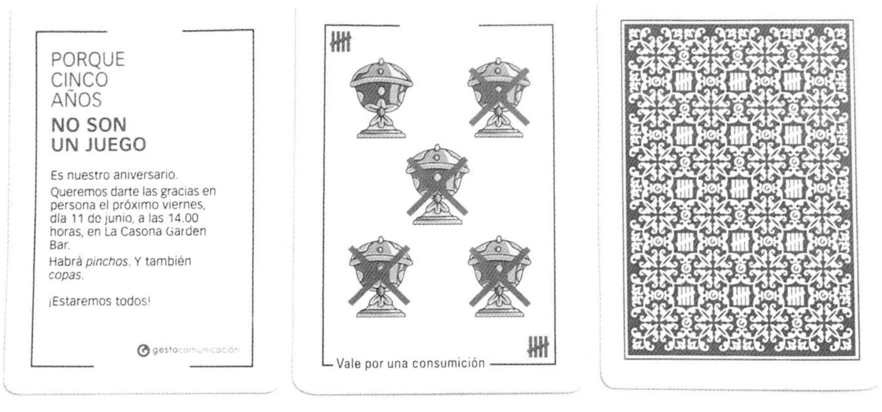
PORQUE
CINCO
AÑOS
NO SON
UN JUEGO
Es nuestro aniversario.
Queremos darte las gracias en persona el próximo viernes, día 11 de junio, a las 14.00 horas, en La Casona Garden Bar.
Habrá pinchos. Y también copas.
¡Estaremos todos!
gestocomunicación
Vale por una consumición

071/
Hey • *Hey's first Christmas greeting. We wanted to highlight the name of the studio and play off the Santa Claus greeting 'Ho, Ho, Ho'.*

072/
ESIETE • *Illuminate 2010. Christmas greetings.*

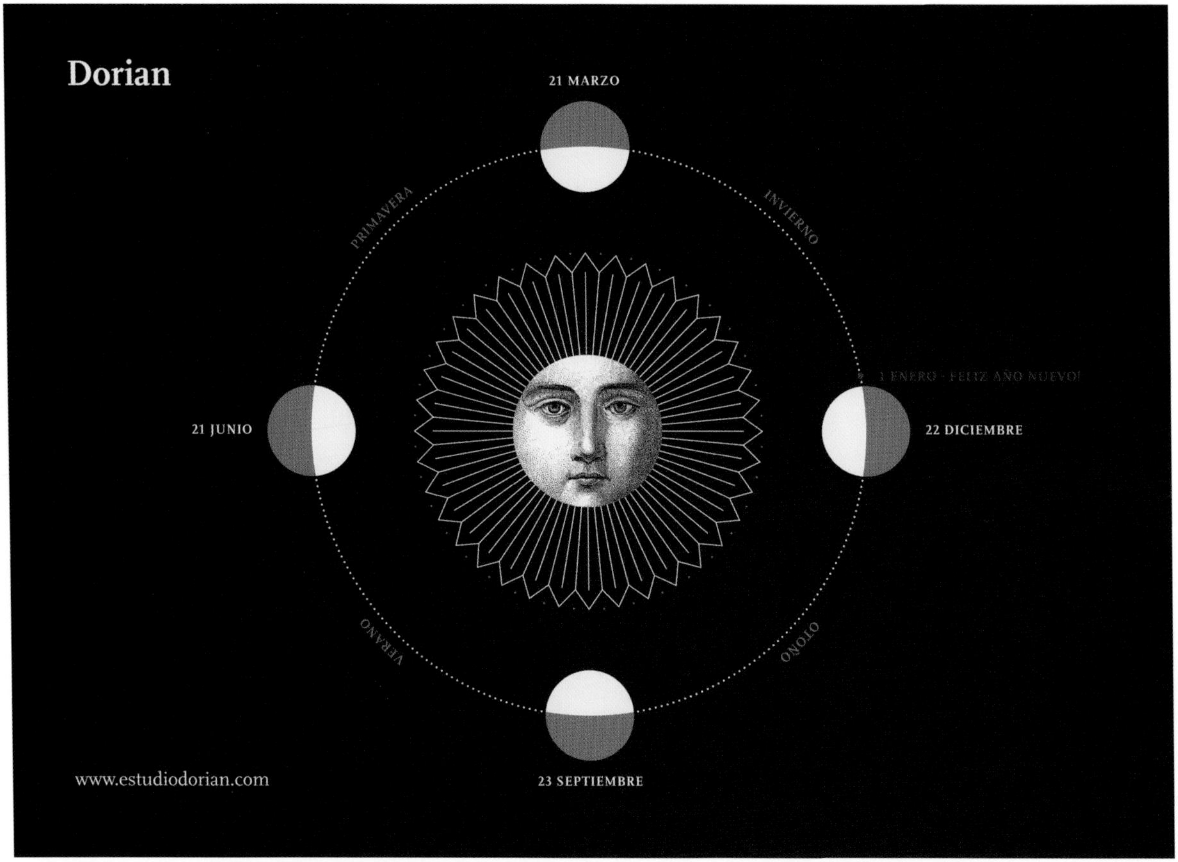

073/
Dorian • *The studio's greetings for 2011.*

074/
Hey • *2010 New Year's Greeting. The idea was to include the number ten of the year represented by a roman numeral.*

HOLA, PRIMAVERA
HOY, SÁBADO 21 DE MARZO DE 2009
TRAE ESTA FLOR A UNA
DE NUESTRAS TIENDAS
Y TE LA CAMBIAMOS
POR UN REGALO
SÓLO UNA FLOR POR PERSONA
ASÍ HABRÁ MÁS REGALOS PARA TODOS
GOYA, 9 ◆ Serrano/Colón
FUENCARRAL, 36 ◆ Gran Vía
MUJI
無印良品

075/

Carlitos y Patricia | Idea Boutique • *During the dawn of March 21st, the first day of spring, 10,000 origami flowers were planted on the streets of Madrid. Anyone coming across one of those flowers could take it to a MUJI store to receive a gift to match the flower. It was a happy day. Spring had arrived.*

MUJI

076/
Sophia Georgopoulou

• *'Plant Your Dreams and Let Them Grow' is the title of Sophia Georgopoulou's self-promotional project and her wish for 2011! The actual tulip flowers and their 'unique' names (e.g., 'Red Emperor', 'Pink Diamond', etc.) inspired the designer to create a series of ecological and interactive packages containing tulip bulbs. The illustrations were inspired by the name of each tulip and were drawn by hand.*

PLANT
YOUR DREAMS
AND LET THEM
GROW!
2011
2 x Red Emperor
Tulip bulb

TIC TAC TIC TAC...

TIC TAC TIC TAC...
ESTO ES LA BOMBA...

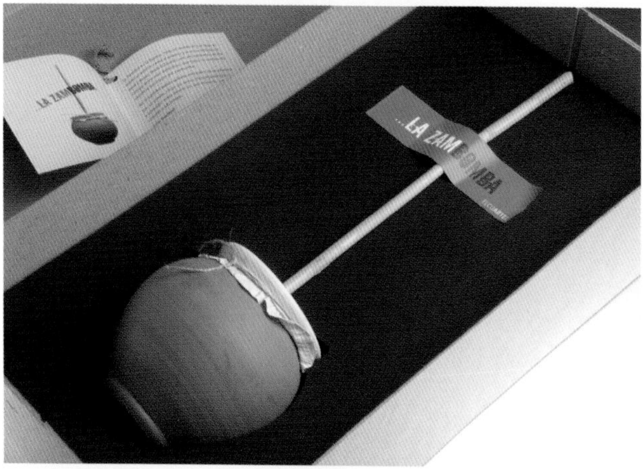
...LA ZAMBOMBA

077/
El Cuartel • *A Christmas package that seems to contain a bomb, but actually contains a drum representing the www.elzambombazo.com.*

078/

Dorian • *Christmas' greetings designed for the model agency, Group Model Management. They define themselves as a big family, so the piece has a naive-style illustration that turns around this same idea, recreating a Christmas tree formed by all the components of the agency.*

Podemos diseñar billetes falsos,
pero esa no es la solución...
La nuestra es ayudarte en tu
negocio, en tus proyectos, dándole
valor a tus productos, mejorando tu
comunicación. Le damos valor a lo
más importante de ti, tú mismo,
tu identidad.
VA77ADAR3S DC
PRÓSP3RO 2010
1000 EURO
BCE ECB EZB EKT EKP
1000
1000 EURO

079/
Valladares Diseño y Comunicación • *1,000 Euro bills for the financial crisis. To greet our clients for 2010, which is in the middle of the economic recession, we sent 1,000 Euro bills which were designed in our studio.*

080/
Seltzer • *Playing off our name, we designed a set of festive drink recipe cards to welcome the New Year. We shot enticing photos of distinctive cocktails and combined them with rich typography to create a promo that's also a keepsake.*

cozy up to 2010!
Stamos
Gin Fizz

CHRISTMAS
RE-IMAGINED
LEVEL 4 • TOWER B • TAKASHIMAYA S.C.
iFOURUM
This Christmas,
surprise and delight your loved ones with a selection of thoughtful and expressive gifts, many lovingly crafted by hand from around the world. Come up to iFourum at Takashimaya Shopping Centre L4 and discover gifts of art that everyone can enjoy.
THE GIFT OF ART
ART FRIEND
BOOKBINDERS DESIGN
CREATIVE HANDS
L'ESCALIER
MERLIN FRAME MAKER & ART GALLERY
STUDIO MIU
THE BETTER GIFT STORE
THE BETTER TOY STORE

081/
&Larry • *This is a Christmas campaign centered on the colorful graphics developed for a Japanesestyle 'furoshiki' fabric wrap giveaway. Each fabric wrapper was presented in an attractive package sealed with a foil-stamped sticker.*

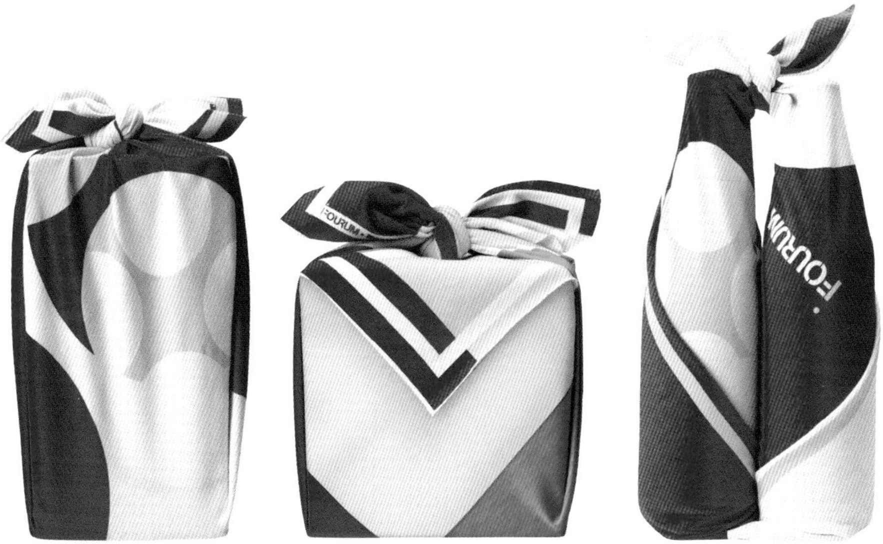
FOURUM
FOURUM

FOURUM

FOURUM

001/ - Promo number
Albertini Romain - Studio name
Club Blister - Client name
France - Country

CLUB BLISTER is a London- and Paris-based collective of DJs, designers, musicians and promoters. - Promo description

036/
ZORRAQUINO
INSSEC, Instituto Sectorial de Promoción y Gestión de Empresas
Spain

A small carton box-Christmas gift, filled with 12 teabags of digestive infusions related to the 12 days of the 'Advent calendar'. Each 'Happy digestion' teabag was prescribed to be enjoyed after the abundant holiday meals of the season (e.g., Christmas Eve dinner, company's Christmas lunch, etc.).

037/
Gorka Aizpurua Serrano
Self-promotion
Spain

Christmas greetings leaflet sent with a magnifying glass, because small details are very often the most important.

038/
Zigurat Comunicación Gráfica, S.L.
Self-promotion
Spain

Our best wishes with a message in a five-panel leaflet that we send to our clients and friends.

039/
KentLyons
Self-promotion
United Kingdom

For our 2009 Christmas card, a 50 cm^2 12-pointed Moravian star, hand-carved from ice, was left to melt over 15 hours. We documented this process with Polaroid film and sent the results out as cards to our friends.

040/
Lucía Castro
Majoral
Spain

The Majoral's Christmas postcard shows the Fiji collection wrapped in vine leaves. The representation and the enclosure try to convey this concept.
Design: Lucía Castro.
Art Director: Martin Azúa.

041/
Carlitos y Patricia | Idea Boutique
5°1ª Salón de Belleza
Spain

More than a simple gift-card, the gift-kits from the 5°1ª Beauty Salon are a present themselves. Besides a personalized beauty treatment, each kit contains a surprise-object: a frog for the Princess kit, a blue paint pastille for the Prince kit and a Swedish crown for the King and Queen kits. Hand-made and printed with a laser printer from low-cost standard material.

042/
take off - media services
Self-promotion
Germany

Development of a promotional tool for our design agency: an extraordinary Christmas mailing filled with polystyrene balls.

043/
Flatland Design
Self-promotion
Portugal

Card sent to Flatland's clients, partners and friends with a New Year's message. Original and playful solution was used to decipher the message, encouraging interaction with the object. The 2010 New Year's card includes a thaumatrope.

044/
take off - media services
Self-promotion
Germany

Development of a promotion-tool for our design agency: an extraordinary Christmasmailing in form of an advent calendar.

045/
SOPA Graphics
Self-promotion
Spain

Christmas greetings. A package of false snow for real people.
Photo: Joan Vicent Cantó.

046/
Carlitos y Patricia | Idea Boutique
MUJI Spain
Spain

What would Santa Claus look like if he were Japanese? He'd be a vending machine. From this idea we built the MUJI Noel Machine, a vending machine to attract customers to the Spanish MUJI stores. The shops were crowded and the action generated buzz in more than 40 countries.

047/
El Cuartel
Artigraf
Spain

Artigraf printers from Malaga celebrated their 25th anniversary. A mailing invitation with three messages.

048/
Sublima Comunicación
Sublima Comunicación
Spain

As the saying goes: 'Snowy year, good year'. Taking into consideration that this enterprise has almost all the clients in Murcia, where it never snows, cork snow was sent to them to wish prosperity during the year.

049/
Flatland Design
Self-promotion
Portugal

Card sent to Flatland's clients, partners, and friends with a New Year's message. Original and playful solution was used to decipher the message, encouraging interaction with the object. The 2009 New Year's card uses solar light.

050/
Uniform
Self-promotion
United Kingdom

An alternative to the usual Christmas card, we created a foil-stamped, typographical 'Closed' sign for clients to hang on their doors as they close shop for the holidays.
Designers: Marcus McCabe and Tim Sharp.

051/
Vertigo Graphix
Self-promotion
Spain

We offer to clients and friends a piece to greet them for Christmas and to give them lots of positive energy in these financially difficult times.
A wink to surprise them.

052/
Maddison Graphic
Self-promotion
United Kingdom

We designed this card to wish our friends and clients a happy Christmas and also to announce our new Website. It is foil blocked black and white on heavy grey board.

053/
Vellut
Self-promotion
Spain

Promotional postcard to greet the New Year. The user can choose the wish that he or she prefers and complete the piece after reading the usual 'Happy New Year 2010'.

054/
Aloof
Realhair
United Kingdom

Christmas card and promotion for the salon's luxury hairdressing service, 'Realhair Privé'.

055/
Pepe Gimeno - Proyecto Gráfico
RNB
Spain

A graphic intervention to create a Christmas'-like atmosphere with cardboard trees in different scales.

056/
Lucía Castro
Lucía Castro
Spain

Go for your wishes in 2010. By completing this a crossword puzzle you find the wishes that you want to fulfil for your new year, such as: happiness, learning, love...

057/
TwoPoints.Net
Col·legi Oficial Disseny Gràfic Catalunya
Spain

TwoPoints.Net has designed the New Year's greetings for the 'Col.legi Oficial Disseny Gràfic Catalunya'. Instead of sending a postcard or chocolates, we wanted to make a useful Christmas gift. And what else is more useful than wrapping paper? The font was specifically designed for this project.

058/
The Creative Method
Self-promotion
Australia

The aim was to create a unique gift to give to our clients at Christmas and to act as a new business introduction. We obtained high-quality cleanskin wines and created our own labels.

059/
StudioCentro Marketing srl
Self-promotion
Italia

There are two ways to face the future: use a talisman or contact a group of professionals like the members of StudioCentro Marketing.

060/
CUBO DISEÑO
Self-promotion
Spain

The most traditional Christmas greeting is a postcard. We wanted to greet our clients in this way, but with a different and very sweet touch.

061/
Edgar Bak
L•A•F PRODUCTION
Poland

10 years' anniversary invitation. Golden pantone on offset paper.

062/
Gorka Aizpurua Serrano
Self-promotion
Spain

Feliz año nueve. Promotional New Year's greeting from the author. Because of the financial crisis he prefers to donate 9 cents to his best friends, which is the cost of the making of a postcard.

063/
extra!
Mercabarna
Spain

A star- shaped greeting leaflet. The idea is to wish a happy New Year showing the Mercabarna day-to-day activities, in daily sequences.

064/
Ryszard Bienert / 3group
Muzeum Sztuki w Łodzi
Poland

New Year's postcard. Brocade and gold foil stamping. Year of publication: December 2010.

065/
Maddison Graphic
Self-promotion
United Kingdom

Our Christmas card for 2010 depicts three ships overprinted on Offenbach bible paper.

066/
Clay McIntosh Creative
Self-promotion
United States

A true 'green' project that uses recycled promo items to create a pop-up Christmas card promotion.

067/
The Creative Method
Self-promotion
Australia

The Creative Method were moving to a new office space, and it was also Christmas time. The idea was to show both.

068/
Menta
Tomás Llavador Arquitectos e Ingenieros
Spain

Season´s greeting card inspired by the geometric structures and surfaces projected in the architectural work of Tomas Llavador.

069/
Nikolaus Schmidt Design
Self-promotion
Austria

Season's greetings for clients and friends.

070/
gestocomunicación
Self-promotion
Spain

A direct campaign mail to promote the 5th anniversary party of gestocomunicación using the message 'Because five years are not a game'.

071/
Hey
Self-promotion
Spain

Hey's first Christmas greeting. We wanted to highlight the name of the studio and play off the Santa Claus greeting 'Ho, Ho, Ho'.

072/
ESIETE
Self-promotion
Spain

Illuminate 2010. Christmas greetings.

073/
Dorian
Dorian
Spain

The studio's greetings for 2011.

074/
Hey
Self-promotion
Spain

2010 New Year's Greeting. The idea was to include the number ten of the year represented by a roman numeral.

075/
Carlitos y Patricia | Idea Boutique
MUJI Spain
Spain

During the dawn of March 21st, the first day of spring, 10,000 origami flowers were planted on the streets of Madrid. Anyone coming across one of those flowers could take it to a MUJI store to receive a gift to match the flower. It was a happy day. Spring had arrived.

076/
Sophia Georgopoulou
Self-promotion Packaging
Greece

'Plant Your Dreams and Let Them Grow' is the title of Sophia Georgopoulou's self-promotional project and her wish for 2011! The actual tulip flowers and their 'unique' names (e.g. ,'Red Emperor', 'Pink Diamond', etc.) inspired the designer to create a series of ecological and interactive packages containing tulip bulbs. The illustrations were inspired by the name of each tulip and were drawn by hand.

077/
El Cuartel
El Cuartel
Spain

A Christmas package that seems to contain a bomb, but actually contains a drum representing the www.elzambombazo.com.

078/
Dorian
Group Model Management
Spain

Christmas' greetings designed for the model agency, Group Model Management. They define themselves as a big family, so the piece has a naive-style illustration that turns around this same idea, recreating a Christmas tree formed by all the components of the agency.

079/
Valladares Diseño y Comunicación
Self-promotion
Spain

1,000 Euro bills for the financial crisis. To greet our clients for 2010, which is in the middle of the economic recession, we sent 1,000 Euro bills which were designed in our studio.

080/
Seltzer
Self-promotion
United States

Playing off our name, we designed a set of festive drink recipe cards to welcome the New Year. We shot enticing photos of distinctive cocktails and combined them with rich typography to create a promo that's also a keepsake.

081/
&Larry
Toshin Development Singapore Pte Ltd
Singapore

This is a Christmas campaign centered on the colorful graphics developed for a Japanesestyle 'furoshiki' fabric wrap giveaway. Each fabric wrapper was presented in an attractive package sealed with a foil-stamped sticker.

To Invite

148 - 189

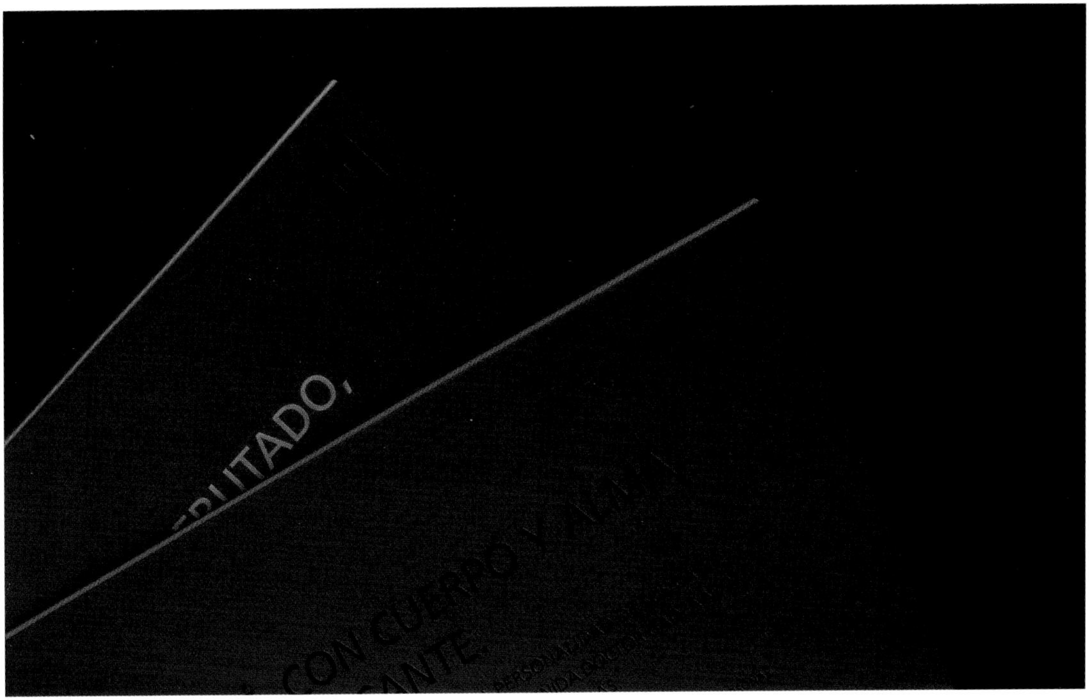

082/
UVE Diseño y Comunicación, S.L. • *Invitation to the official opening of Alicante's Boutique. The mailing consists of a red envelope with black stamping, and a black laminated invitation with red paper inside. The main characteristics of Nespresso's 16 coffee varieties are listed with 16 different gloss stampings which suggest the colours of the respective capsules.*

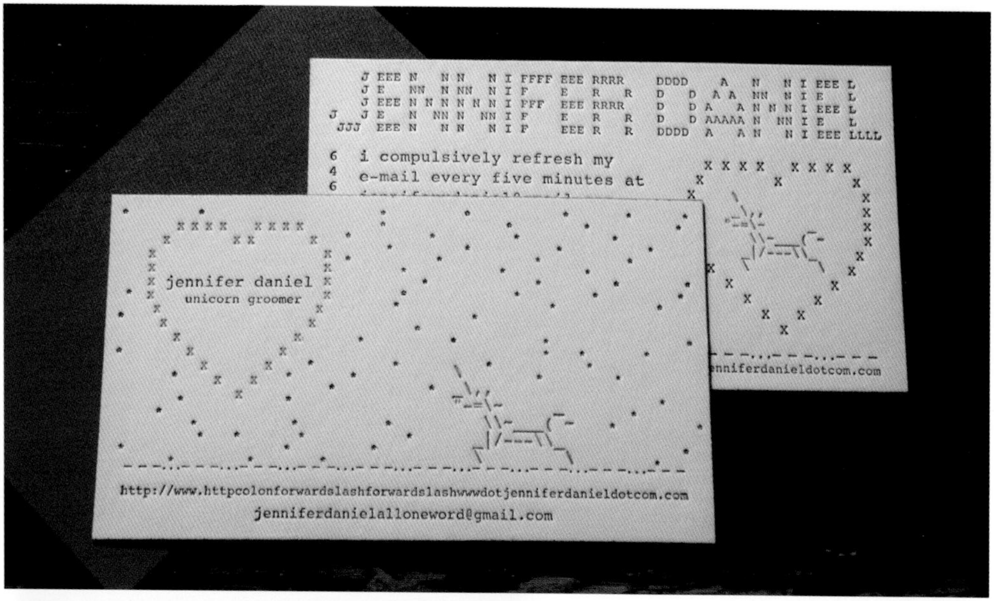

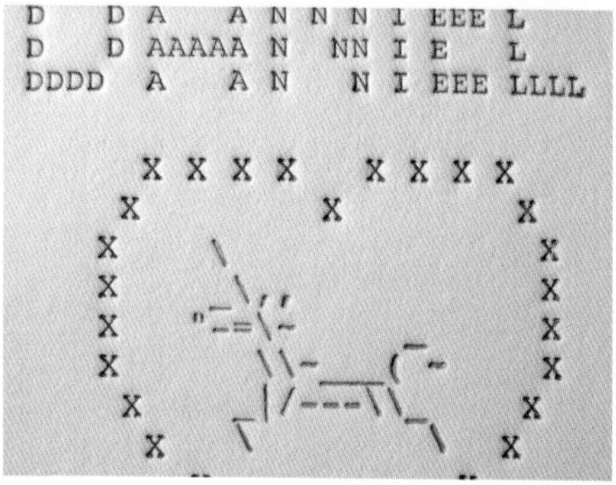

083/
Jennifer Daniel • *Jennifer Daniel business cards.*

084/

Fabien Barral • *'Harmonie intérieure' is our online shop. We choose a small but tactile card versus a large run offset flyer to invite 100 people to attend a trade show.*

El dia 4 d'octubre de 2008...

...serà el més dolç de la nostra vida
sònia i albert

085/
Gorka Aizpurua Serrano • *Sonia and Albert invite you to share their sweetest day with a sweet heart-shaped lollipop.*

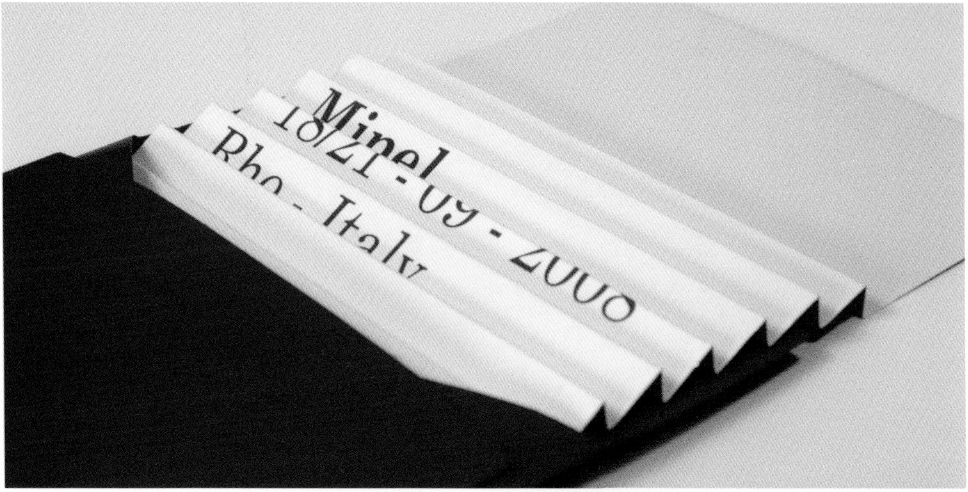

086/
jekyll & hyde • *Invitation cards for 'RH' milano brand.*

LOVE LETTERS
JORGE & KATYA
JK
ALMEIDA & BAUVAL
AB
ALWAYS TOGETHER
ABCDEFG
HIJKLMN
OPQRST
UVWXYZ
ON SATURDAY THE 28TH
OF SEPTEMBER AT 7.30PM
WE WILL BE CELEBRATING
OUR MARRIAGE AT THE
HACIENDA MORENO IN
ALHAURIN EL GRANDE
CLOSE TO MALAGA, SPAIN

087/
Neil Cutler Design • *Jorge Almeida and Katya Bauval wedding invitation. The solution for this design comes from the initials JK and AB and their relationship in the alphabet.*

SOME
TIMES

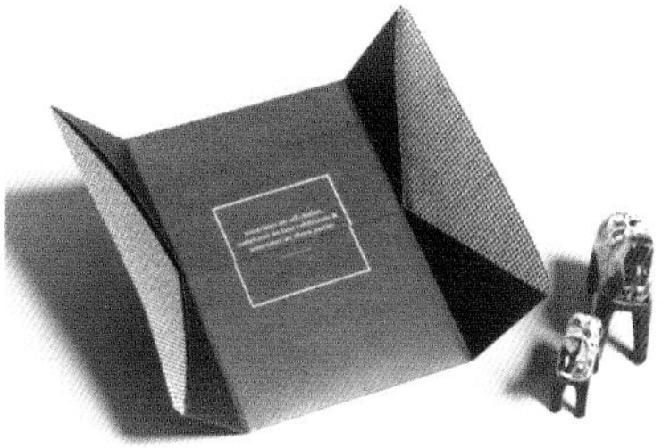

088/
James Kape • *This was an invitation created as a form of promotion for the launch of the magazine 'Sometimes'.*

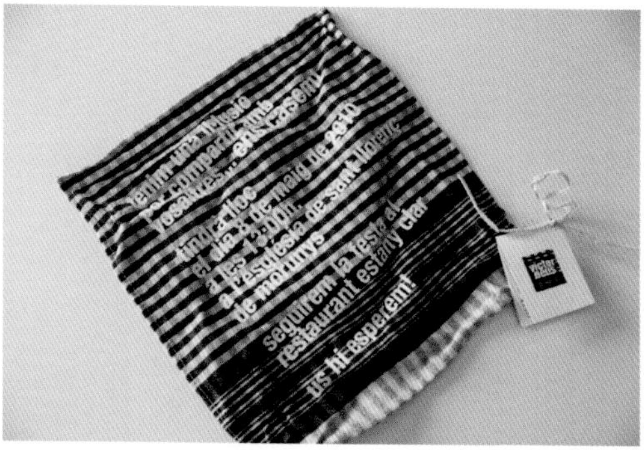

089/
Esther Barniol / Projectes Creatius • *The aim was to communicate with the wedding invitation the casual and rustic atmosphere of the event.*

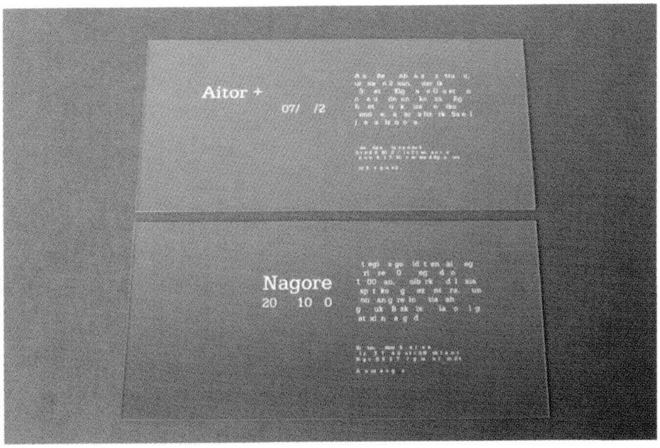

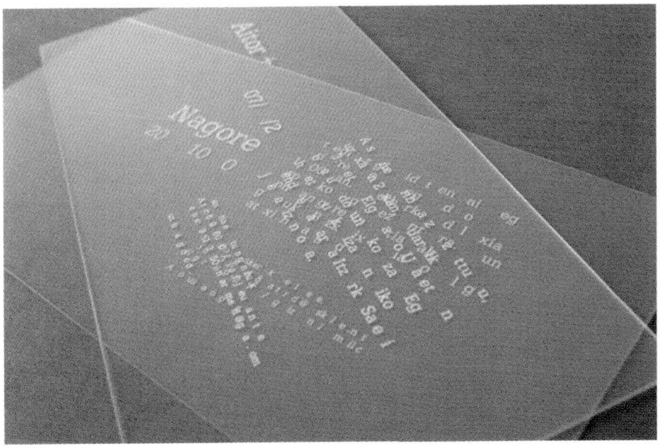

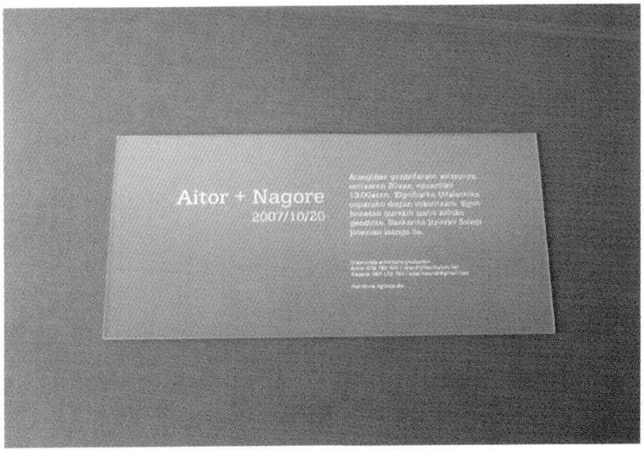

090/
la caja de tipos • *In a wedding, two persons are united by marriage. We wanted this concept to be present, so we separated the texts in letters and put them in two transparent acetates.*

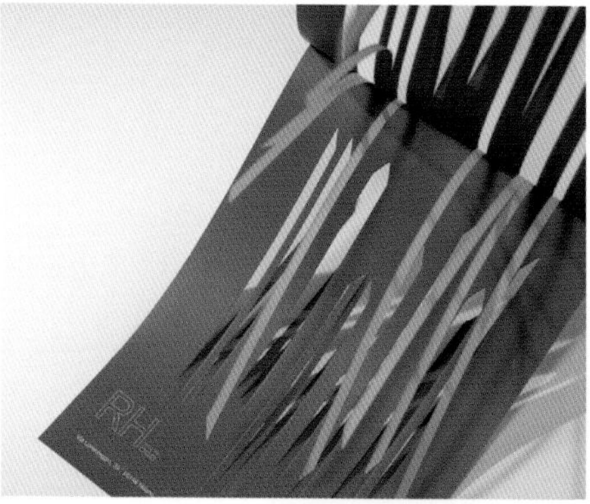

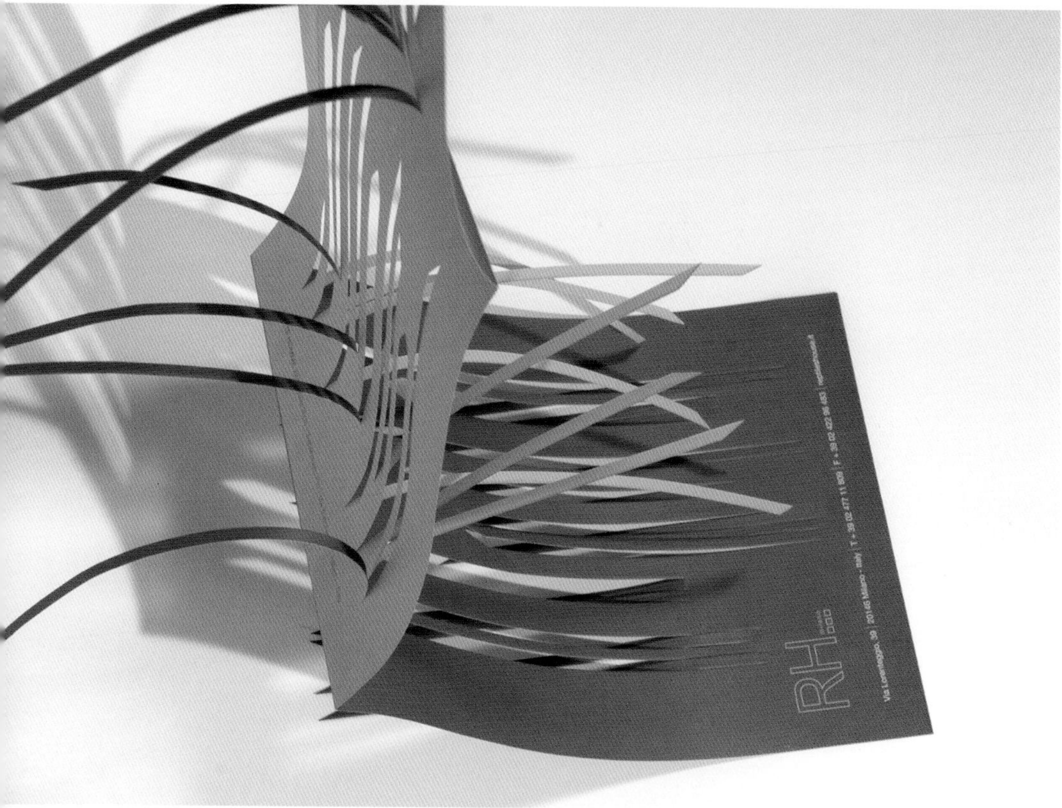

091/
jekyll & hyde • *For 'RH Milano' we designed the invitation cards for their new collection of handbags. The design was inspired by the vertical gardens, modern review of the Babylonian roof gardens.*

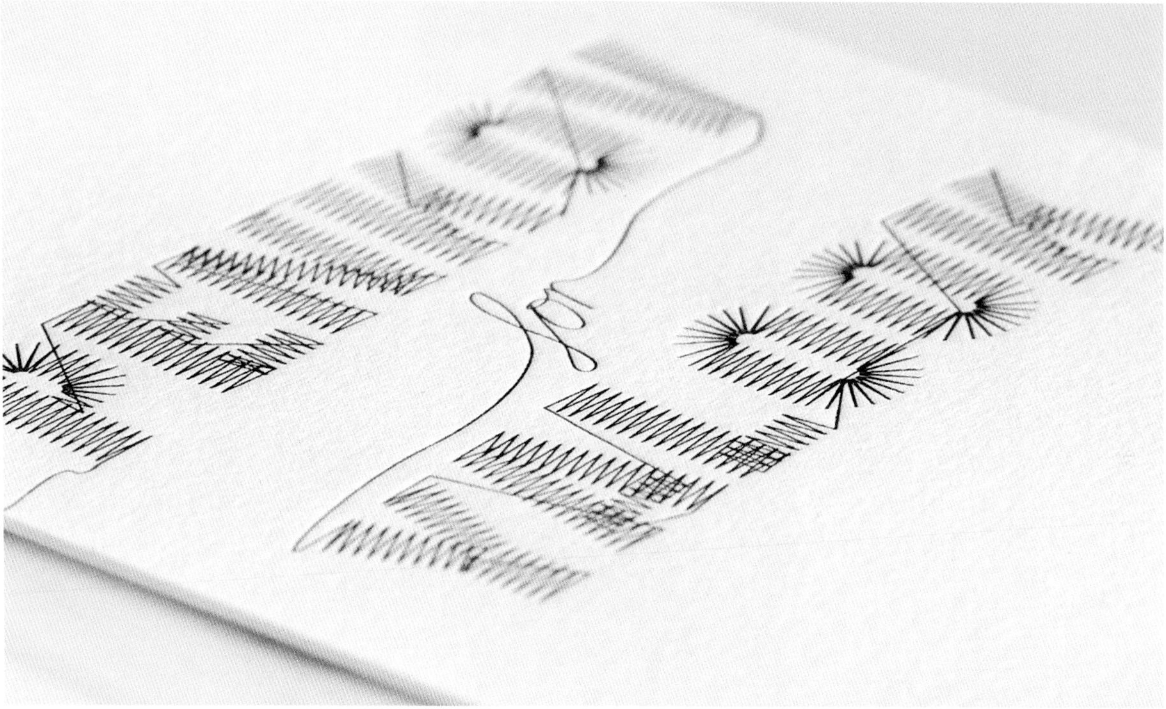

092/
H2D2, Visual Communications • *Fashion designer in Penkov presented two new dresses during the Fashion Week 2010 in Berlin. We designed the logo and the invitation card for the event.*

PENKOV
for
YALOOK
www.yalook.com

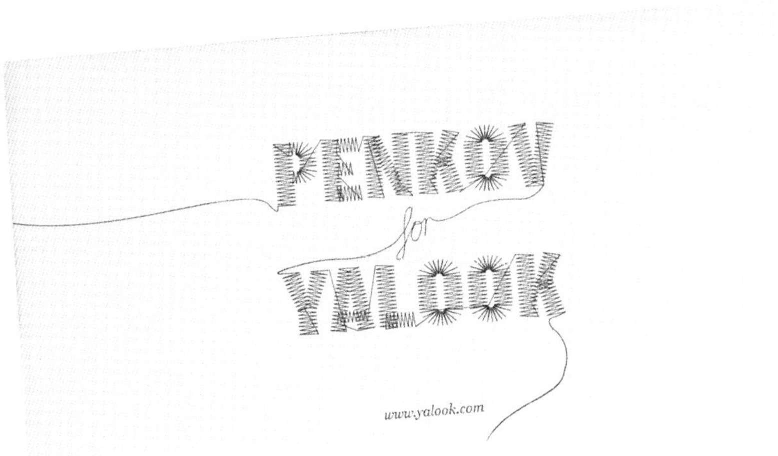
PENKOV
for
YALOOK
www.yalook.com

093/
jekyll & hyde • *Invitation card for 'combines', an art design gallery.*

combines
creatività urbana
artisti impuri
carrus
scultrice
designer
alberto clementi
architetto
fotografo
alberto cucchi
disoccupato
intagliatore
fabrizio dusi
artista
ceramista
valeria nevola
studentessa
fotografa

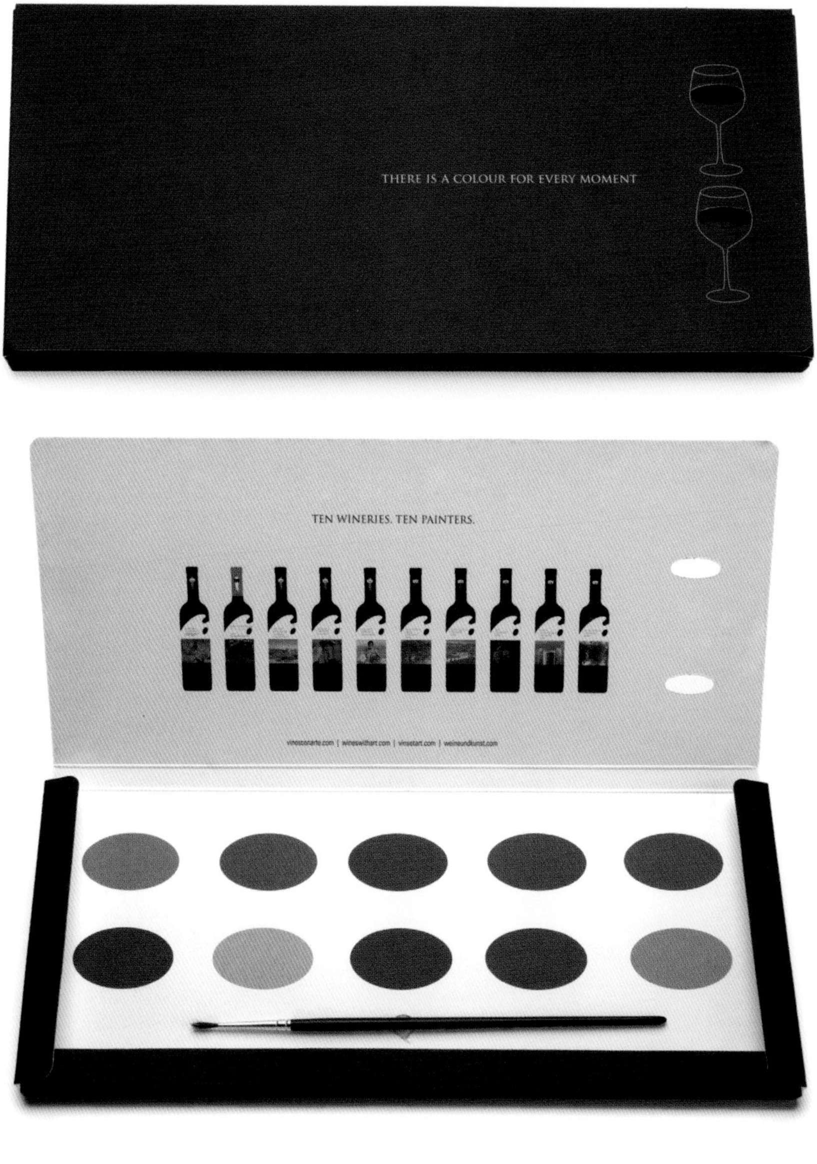

094/
El Cuartel • *Invitation to the Conarte presentation (a wine selection that links 10 wine cellars to 10 painters of Malaga) for journalists and wine tasters of different countries.*

Si!

Simc!

Simone & Ramón
...zullen gaan trouwen op 12 juni 2003 in Barcelona en je bent/jullie zijn van harte uitgenodigd om dit samen met ons te vieren
...celebrarán su boda el día 12 de junio 2003 en Barcelona y estariamos encantados de contar con tu/vuestra presencia
...are getting married on the 12th of June 2003 in Barcelona and we'd love you to come and celebrate this day with us

095/
Neil Cutler Design • *Simone Sholtz and Ramón Rodriguez's wedding invitation. Simone says 'yes' to Ramon.*

096/
Dorian • *Wedding invitation that focuses on the most significant element of the union: the alliance. Built through a universe inspired by the ornamental iconography of the 19th century, the illustrations of this alliance represent the most characteristic aspects of the couple.*

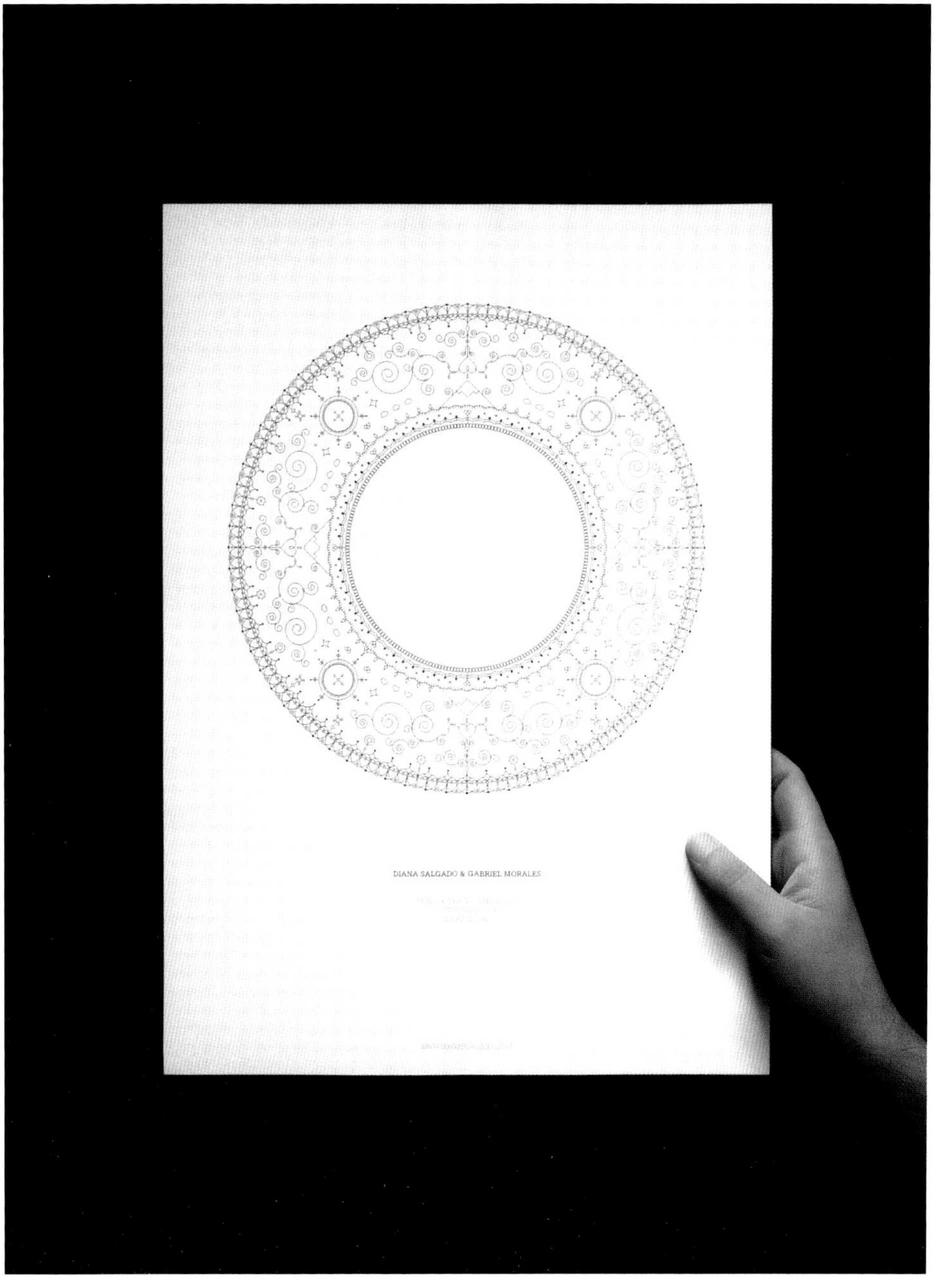
DIANA SALGADO & GABRIEL MORALES

097/
Neil Cutler Design • *A card to communicate Boyd's birth, first announcing that he was a boy and then by spelling out his name.*

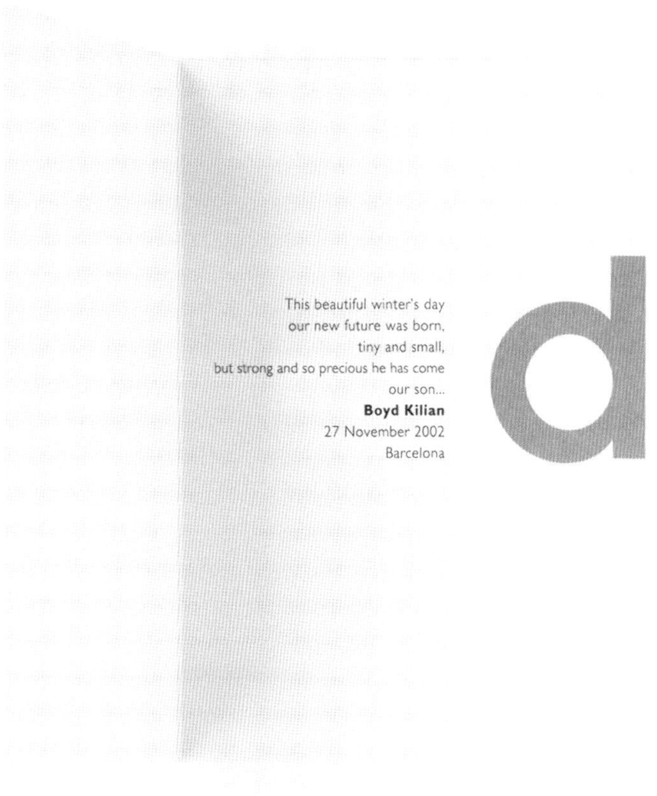
This beautiful winter's day
our new future was born,
tiny and small,
but strong and so precious he has come
our son...
Boyd Kilian
27 November 2002
Barcelona
d

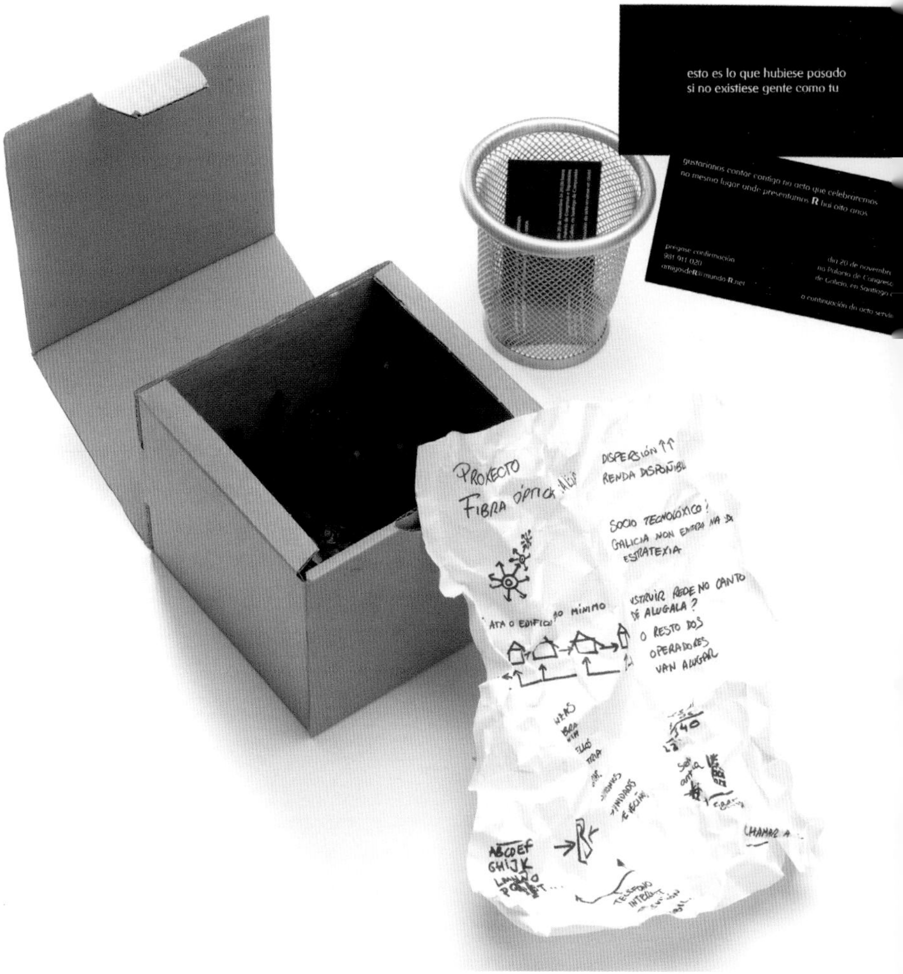

098/
Quattro idcp • *Invitation to the 8th anniversary of 'R enterprise', galician cable operators.*

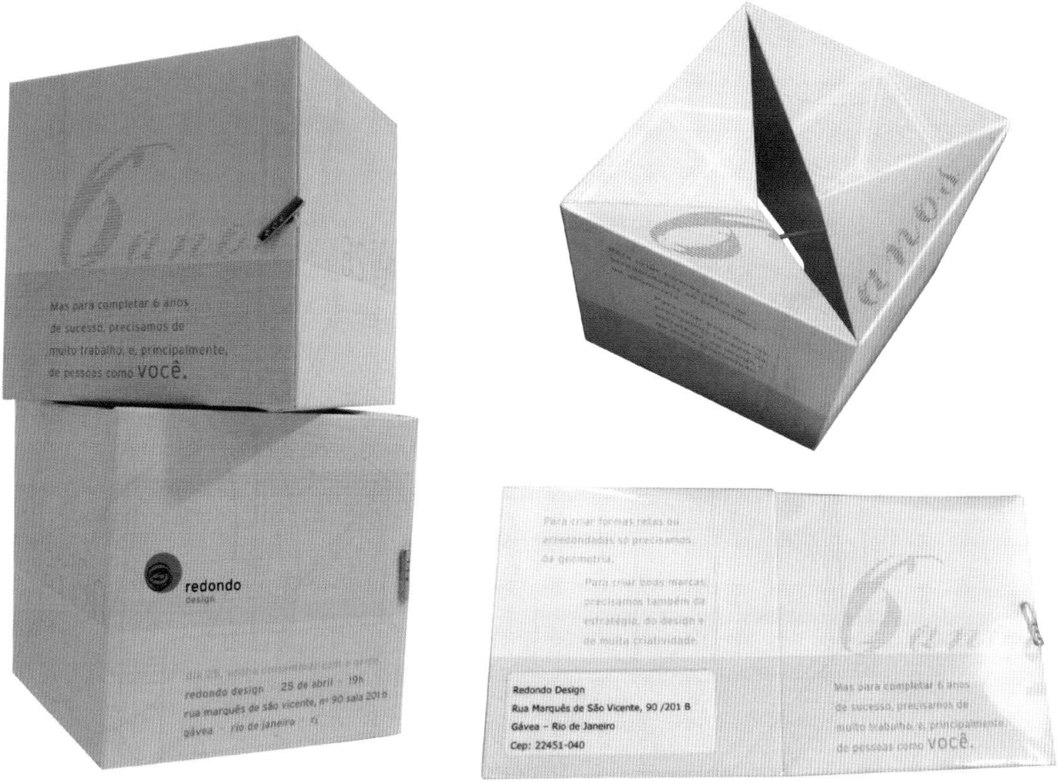

099/
redondo design • *In the jargon of design in Brazil, redondo means 'no edges': a metaphor we use to express a feeling that arises when the work reaches its most perfect form.*

Trapped in Suburbia • *With the 'Gotcha!' project, or 'Hebbes!' in Dutch,, museumgoudA is one of the few museums in the world to take the first steps towards liberating their historic heritage collections into the 3D scan medium for all to view.*

UITNODIGING

UITNODIGING

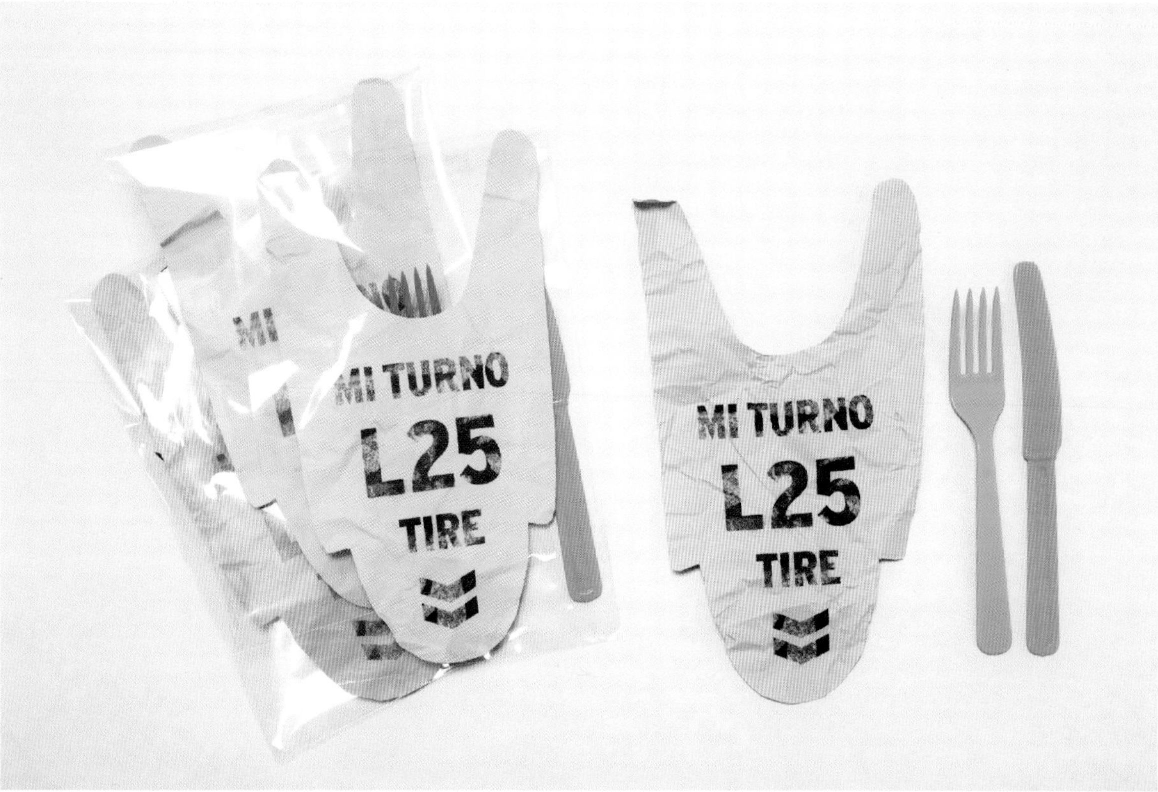

101/
Lucía Castro • *This is the invitation I created for my 25th brithday. Never better said - My turn 25 years -. The invitation comes with a table-set to enjoy a day of BBQ. In order to get your meal, you had to show your turn.*

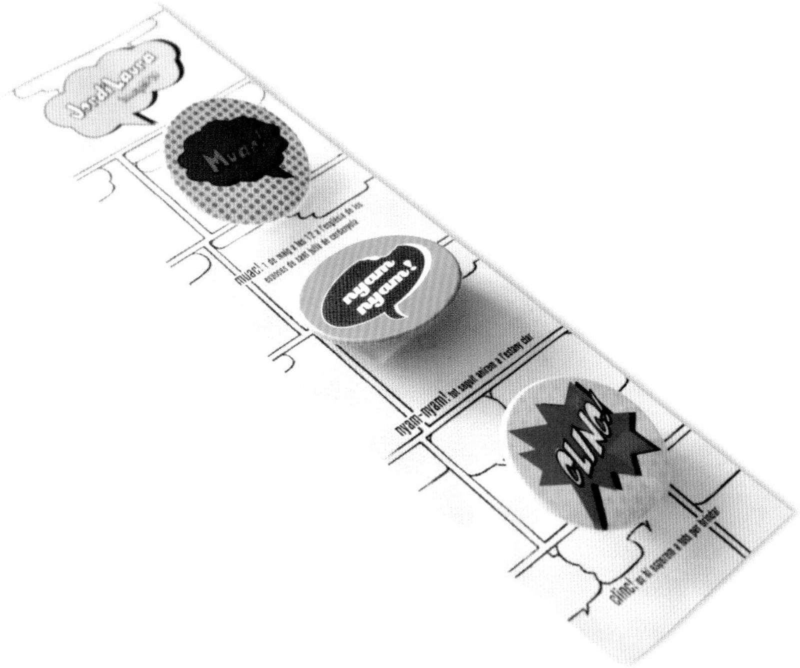

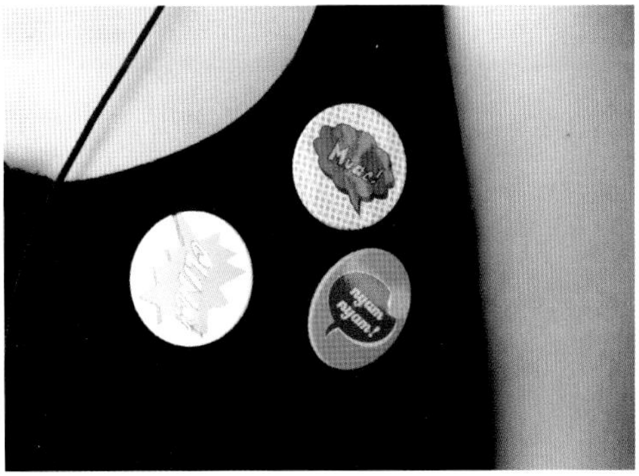

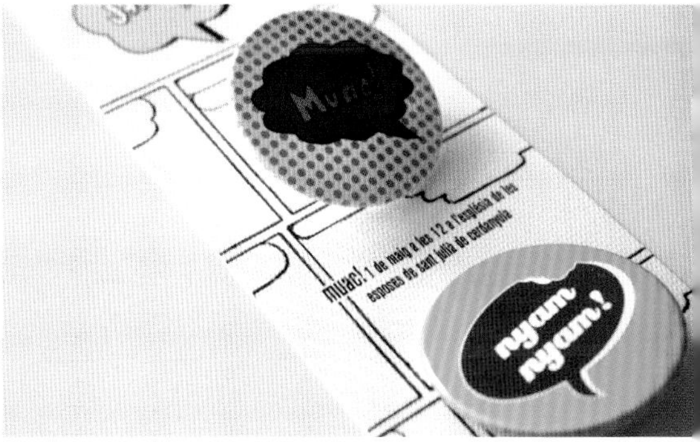

102/
Esther Barniol / Projectes Creatius • *Invitation linked to the comic strip world as the wedding itself. The guests took part of and understood the funny premise of the party.*

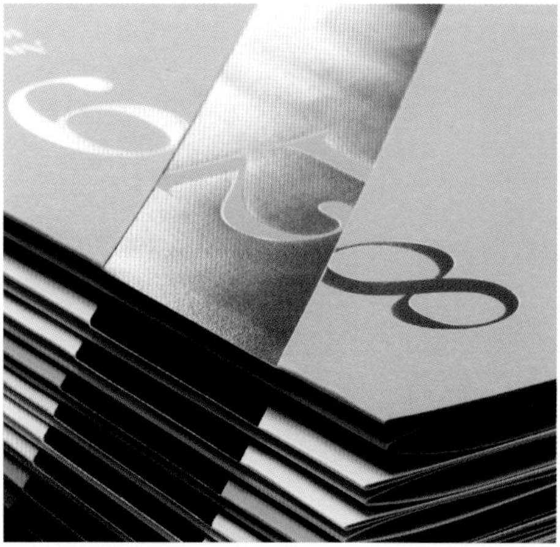

103/
Design LSC • *Invitation to an event promoting the new 'Fedrigoni Sirio Collection'. Inspired by the many different and intense colours contained in the range.*

8
12
9
An invitation to view the latest edition of Imaginative Papers.

8
2
9
8
2
9
Different ranges in one single swatch
8
2
9
Different ranges in one single swatch

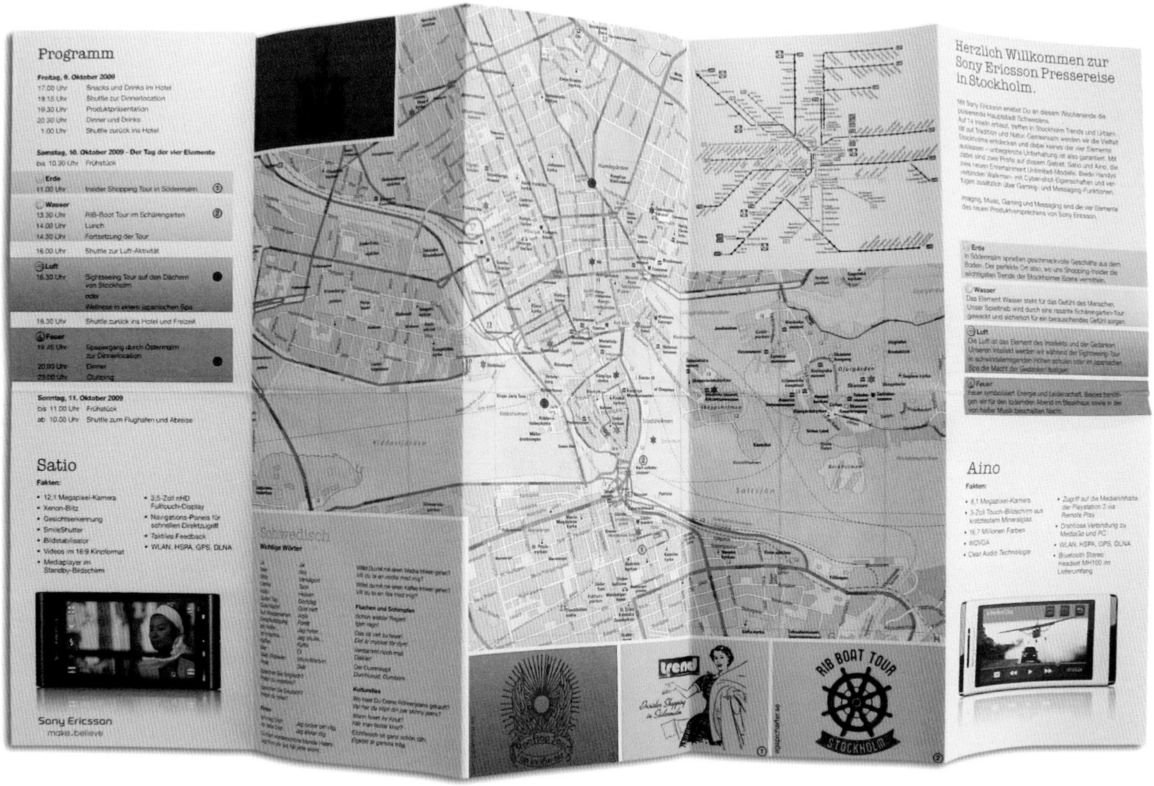

104/
Melville Brand Design • *Invitation for a press event in Stockholm. Sony Ericsson categorizes the feature of its mobile phones 'Aino' and 'Saito' and links each feature with the four elements.*

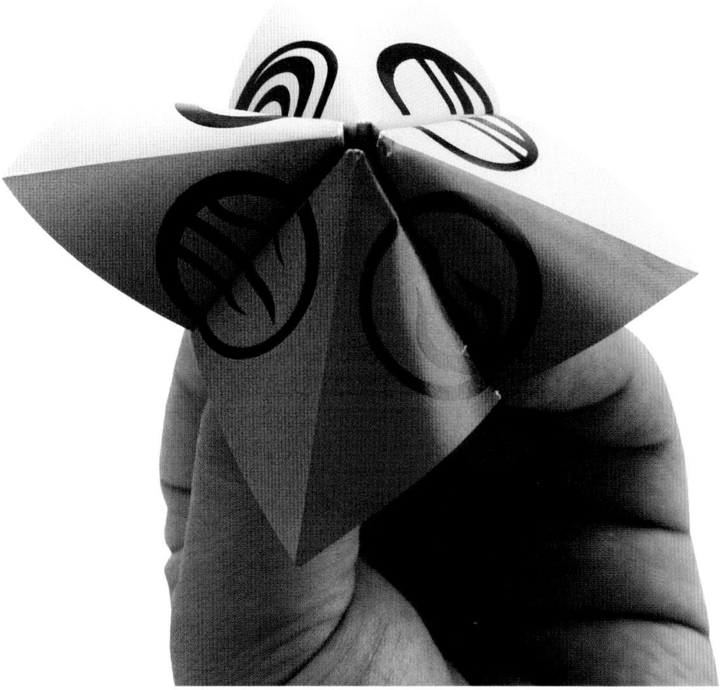

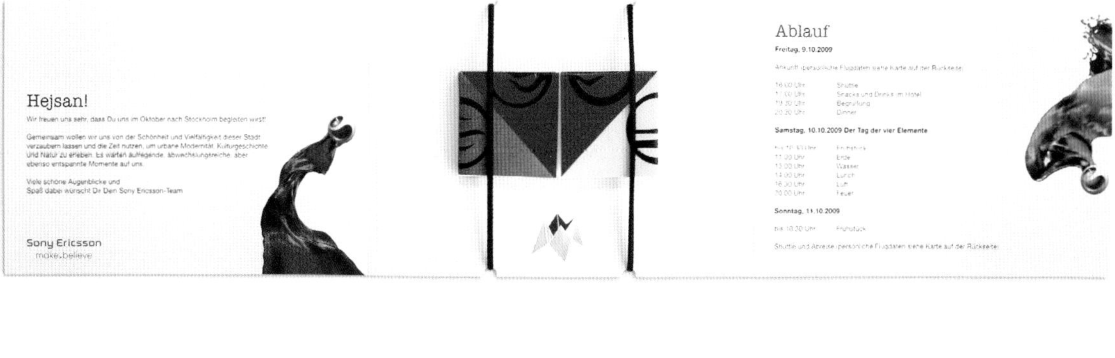
Hejsan!
Wir freuen uns sehr, dass Du uns im Oktober nach Stockholm begleiten wirst!
Gemeinsam wollen wir uns von der Schönheit und Vielfältigkeit dieser Stadt verzaubern lassen und die Zeit nutzen, um urbane Modernität, Kulturgeschichte und Natur zu erleben. Es warten aufregende, abwechslungsreiche, aber ebenso entspannte Momente auf uns.
Viele schöne Augenblicke und
Spaß dabei wünscht Dir Dein Sony Ericsson-Team
Sony Ericsson
make.believe
Ablauf
Freitag, 9.10.2009
Shuttle
Snacks und Drinks im Hotel
Begrüßung
Dinner
Samstag, 10.10.2009 Der Tag der vier Elemente
11.00 Uhr
Erde
Wasser
Lunch
Luft
Feuer
Sonntag, 11.10.2009
Frühstück
Shuttle und Abreise (persönliche Flugdaten siehe Karte auf der Rückseite)

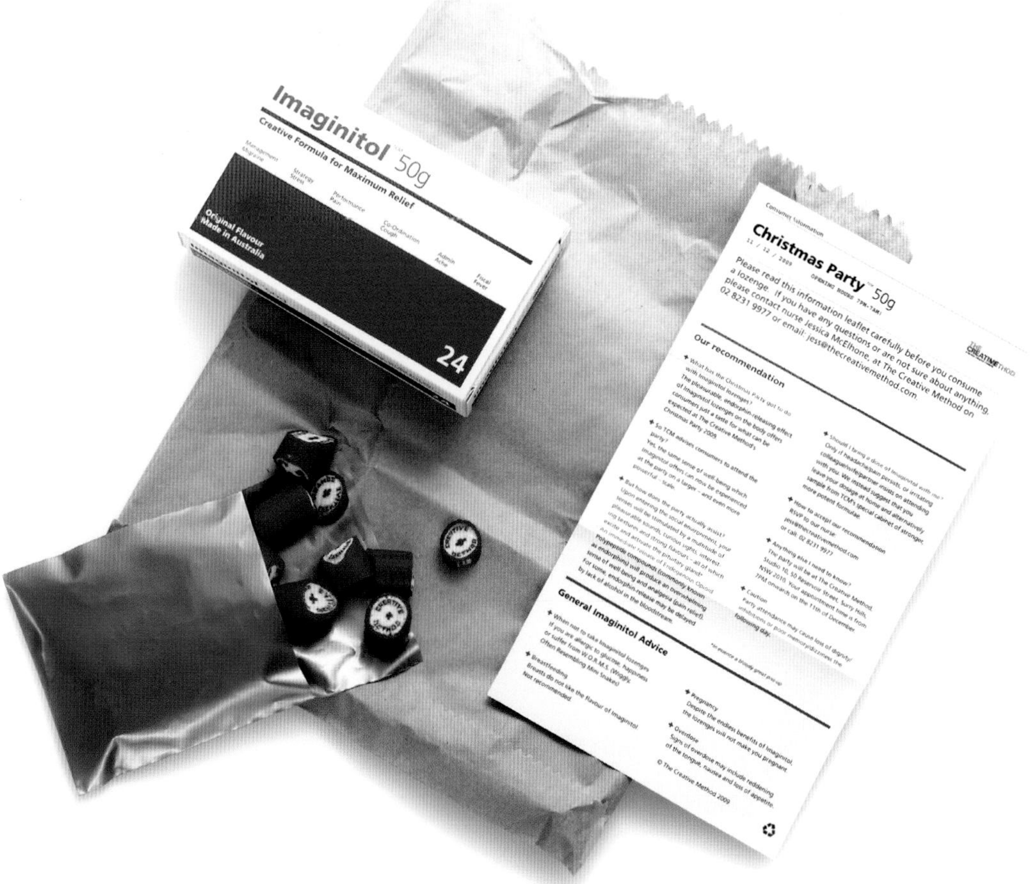

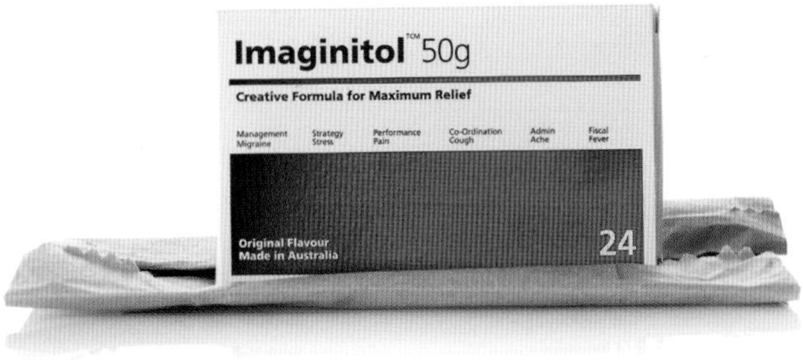

105/

The Creative Method • *The brief was to create an interesting and engaging invitation to The Creative Method Xmas party. It needed to illustrate what we do, but also create a high level of interest and anticipation for the party.*

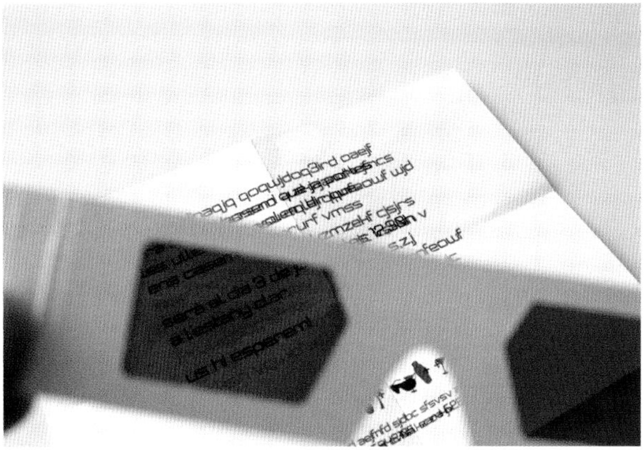

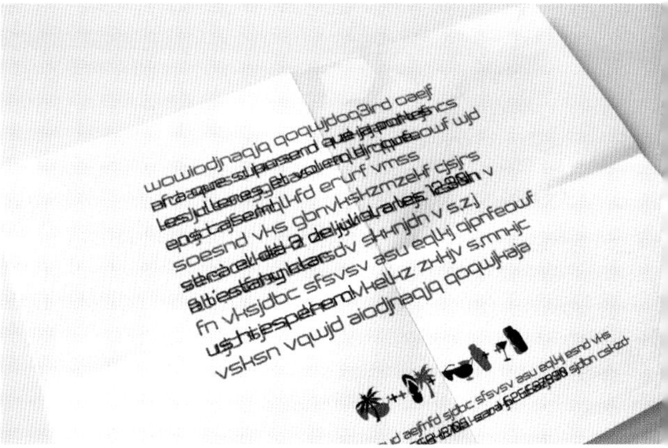

106/
Esther Barniol / Projectes Creatius • *The aim was to communicate with the invitation the beach party atmosphere of the event.*

001/ - Promo number
Albertini Romain - Studio name
Club Blister - Client name
France - Country

CLUB BLISTER is a London- and Paris-based collective of DJs, designers, musicians and promoters. - Promo description

082/
UVE Diseño y Comunicación, S.L.
Nespresso
Spain

Invitation to the official opening of Alicante's Boutique. The mailing consists of a red envelope with black stamping, and a black laminated invitation with red paper inside. The main characteristics of Nespresso's 16 coffee varieties are listed with 16 different gloss stampings which suggest the colours of the respective capsules.

083/
Jennifer Daniel
Self-promotion
United States

Jennifer Daniel business cards.

084/
Fabien Barral
Harmonie intérieure
France

'Harmonie intérieure' is our online shop. We choose a small but tactile card versus a large run offset flyer to invite 100 people to attend a trade show.

085/
Gorka Aizpurua Serrano
Sonia y Albert
Spain

Sonia and Albert invite you to share their sweetest day with a sweet heart-shaped lollipop.

086/
jekyll & hyde
RH milano
Italy

Invitation cards for 'RH milano' brand.

087/
Neil Cutler Design
Jorge Almeida and Katya Bauval
Spain

Jorge Almeida and Katya Bauval wedding invitation. The solution for this design comes from the initials JK and AB and their relationship in the alphabet.

088/
James Kape
Some Agency
Australia

This was an invitation created as a form of promotion for the launch of the magazine 'Sometimes'.

089/
Esther Barniol / Projectes Creatius
Restaurante Estany Clar
Spain

The aim was to communicate with the wedding invitation the casual and rustic atmosphere of the event.

090/
la caja de tipos
Aitor and Nagore
Spain

In a wedding, two persons are united by marriage. We wanted this concept to be present, so we separated the texts in letters and put them in two transparent acetates.

091/
jekyll & hyde
RH milano
Italy

For 'RH Milano' we designed the invitation cards for their new collection of handbags. The design was inspired by the vertical gardens, modern review of the Babylonian roof gardens.

092/
H2D2, Visual Communications
Fashionworld GmbH
Germany

Fashion designer in Penkov presented two new dresses during the Fashion Week 2010 in Berlin. We designed the logo and the invitation card for the event.

093/
jekyll & hyde
combines
Italy

Invitation card for 'combines', an art design gallery.

094/
El Cuartel
Málaga Conarte
Spain

Invitation to the Conarte presentation (a wine selection that links 10 wine cellars to 10 painters of Malaga) for journalists and wine tasters of different countries.

095/
Neil Cutler Design
Simone Scholtz and Ramón Rodríguez
Spain

Simone Sholtz and Ramón Rodriguez´s wedding invitation. Simone says 'yes' to Ramon.

096/
Dorian
Diana & Gabriel
Spain

Wedding invitation that focuses on the most significant element of the union: the alliance. Built through a universe inspired by the ornamental iconography of the 19th century, the illustrations of this alliance represent the most characteristic aspects of the couple.

097/
Neil Cutler Design
Charles van den Berg and Alexandra Dekker
Spain

A card to communicate Boyd's birth, first announcing that he was a boy and then by spelling out his name.

098/
Quattro idcp
R, cable y telecomunicaciones
Spain

Invitation to the 8th anniversary of 'R enterprise', galician cable operators.

099/
redondo design
Self-promotion
Brazil

In the jargon of design in Brazil, redondo means 'no edges': a metaphor we use to express a feeling that arises when the work reaches its most perfect form.

100/
Trapped in Suburbia
Museum Gouda
The Netherlands

With the 'Gotcha!' project, or 'Hebbes!' in Dutch,, museumgoudA is one of the few museums in the world to take the first steps towards liberating their historic heritage collections into the 3D scan medium for all to view.

101/
Lucía Castro
Lucía Castro
Spain

This is the invitation I created for my 25th brithday. Never better said - My turn 25 years -. The invitation comes with a table-set to enjoy a day of BBQ. In order to get your meal, you had to show your turn.

102/
Esther Barniol / Projectes Creatius
Restaurant Estany Clar
Spain

Invitation linked to the comic strip world as the wedding itself. The guests took part of and understood the funny premise of the party.

103/
Design LSC
Fedrigoni UK
United Kingdom

Invitation to an event promoting the new 'Fedrigoni Sirio Collection'. Inspired by the many different and intense colours contained in the range.

104/
Melville Brand Design
Sony Ericsson
Germany

Invitation for a press event in Stockholm. Sony Ericsson categorizes the feature of its mobile phones 'Aino' and 'Saito' and links each feature with the four elements.

105/
The Creative Method
Self-promotion
Australia

The brief was to create an interesting and engaging invitation to The Creative Method Xmas party. It needed to illustrate what we do, but also create a high level of interest and anticipation for the party.

106/
Esther Barniol / Projectes Creatius
Restaurant Estany Clar
Spain

The aim was to communicate with the invitation the beach party atmosphere of the event.

To sell

190 - 303

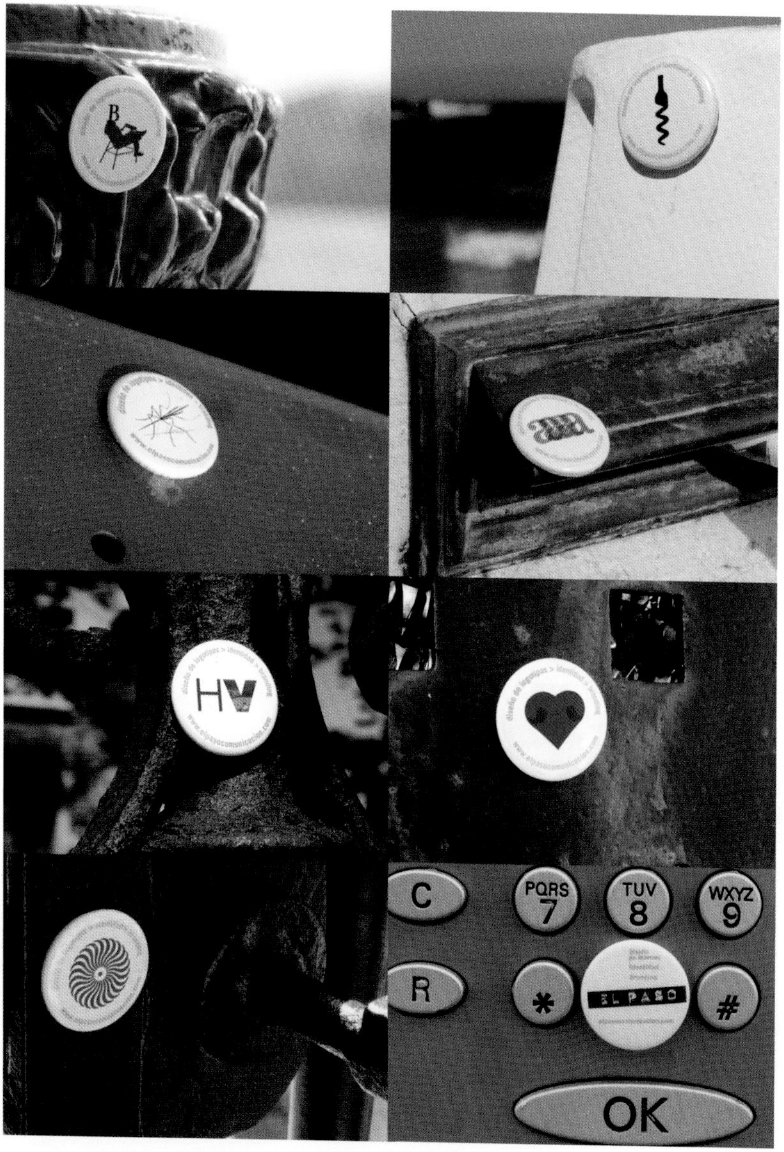

107/
El Paso, Galería de Comunicación • *'We are our projects'. At El Paso we are our logos. With this philosophy, we design magnets to point out the nature of our work.*

Para gustos.... COLORES
TOMATES AZULES

108/
VisioGlobal • *For tastes, colours. Promotional element for 'Tomates azules'.*

109/
ATIPUS • *To entertain your peaceful moments during the summer holidays, we recreated the mythic game 'Battleship', in two pocket notebooks; neither electricity nor Internet connections are required!*

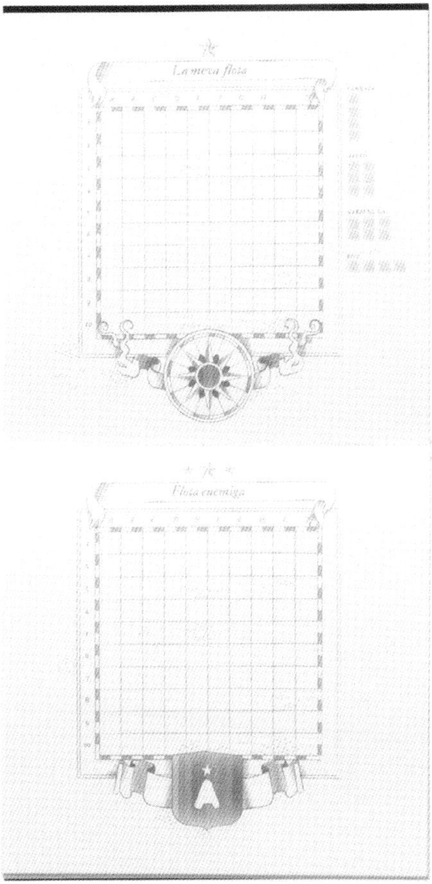
La meva flota
Flota enemiga

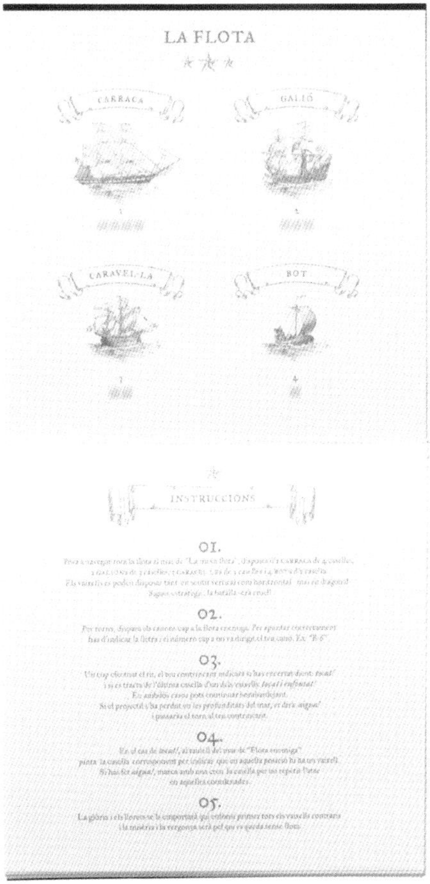
LA FLOTA
CARRACA
GALIÓ
CARAVEL·LA
BOT
INSTRUCCIONS
01.
02.
03.
04.
05.

110/
Bisgràfic • *Promotional tee-shirts for Bryks, an on line brand for design's objects.*

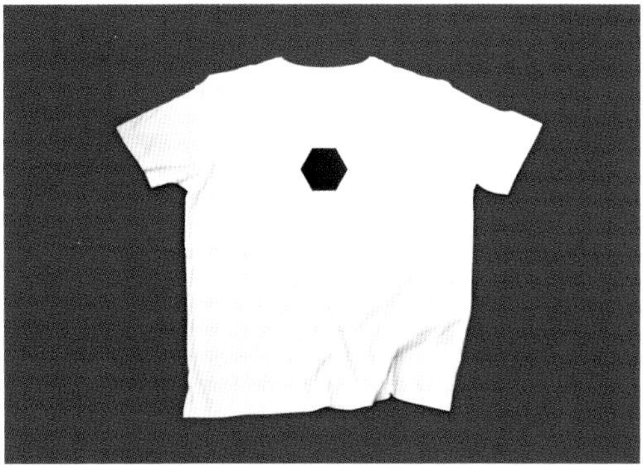
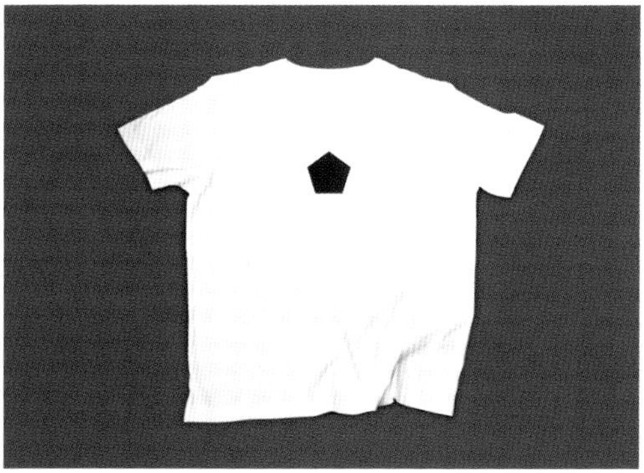
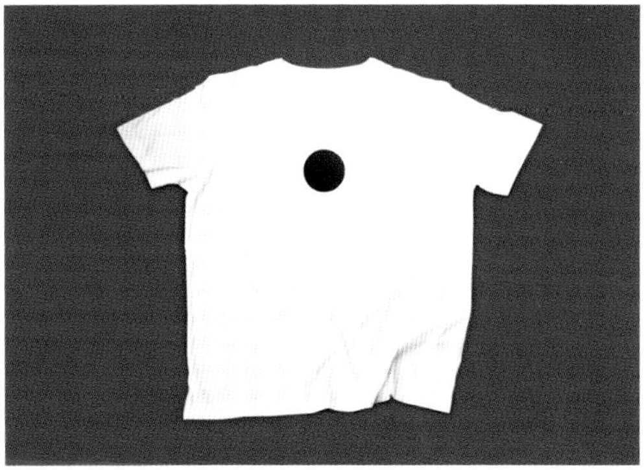
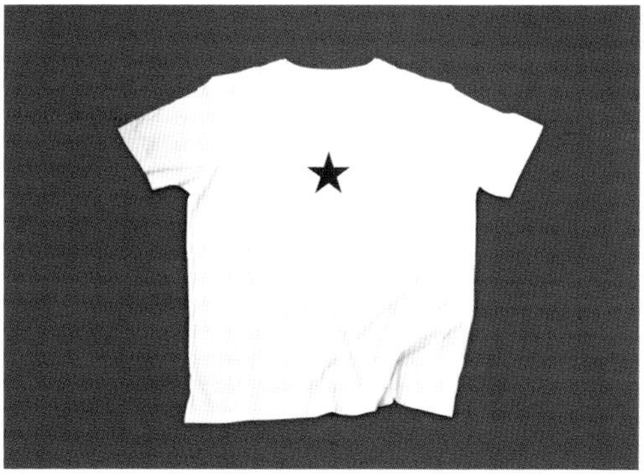
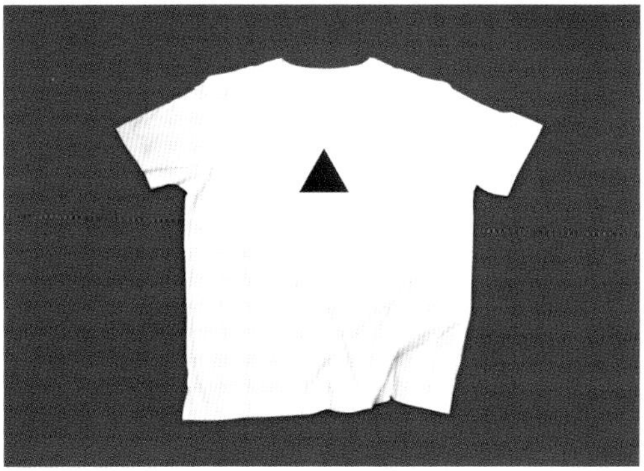
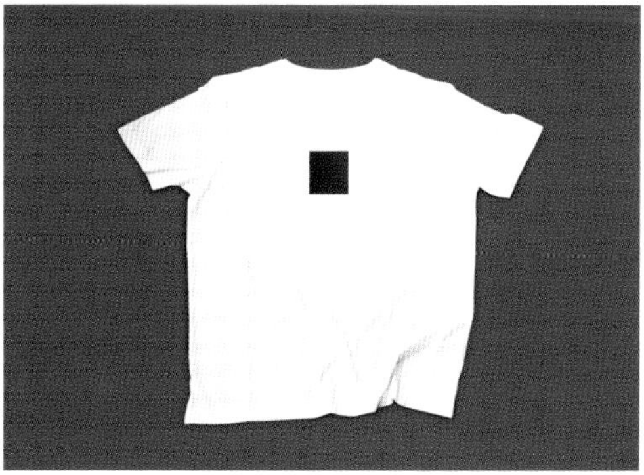

¡Ei! Por favor
Sácame de aquí
Me falta el oxígeno
SANDWICHDEBOOK
1.400gr
TINTA: BLANCO Y NEGRO
CONTENIDO: ESENCIA DE SANDWICH
RESUMEN VITAL DE LO QUE PODEMOS
HACER POR TU MARCA
SAN
DWI
CH
ESTO NO ES
UN SANDWICH
EN BREVE
NOS PROBARÁS
QUEREMOS
RECORDARTE QUE
EN UNOS DÍAS
TENDREMOS UNA CITA
Bon appétit
SAN
DWI
CH

111/
Sandwich • *Sandwich's picnic. Corporate and promotional campaign.*

ESTO NO ES
UN SANDWICH
WWW.SANDWI
CHDEWEB.COM
MOLT AVIAT
ENS TASTARÀS
SAN
DWI
CH

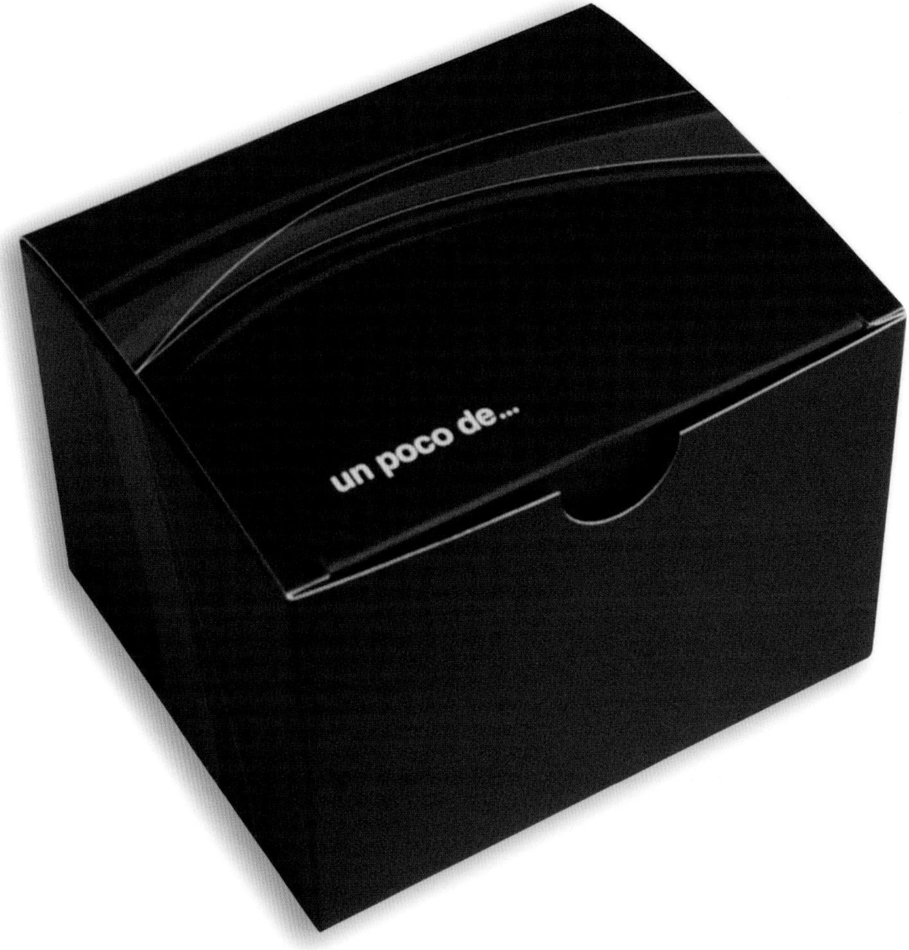

112/
Virbia • *Promotional mailing to capture the attention of new clients.*

aire
fresco
aire
fresco

aire
fresco

Consultants Grupa
Trakošćanska 4
10 000 Zagreb
T 01 3037 300
www.consultants.hr
2010

2010
2010

113/
Bunch • *For two years in a row, we helped the Consultants real estate investors start the New Year with new collateral. In 2010 a screen-printed planner in an edition of 200 was produced along with a newly designed calendar and colorful range of Christmas cards.*

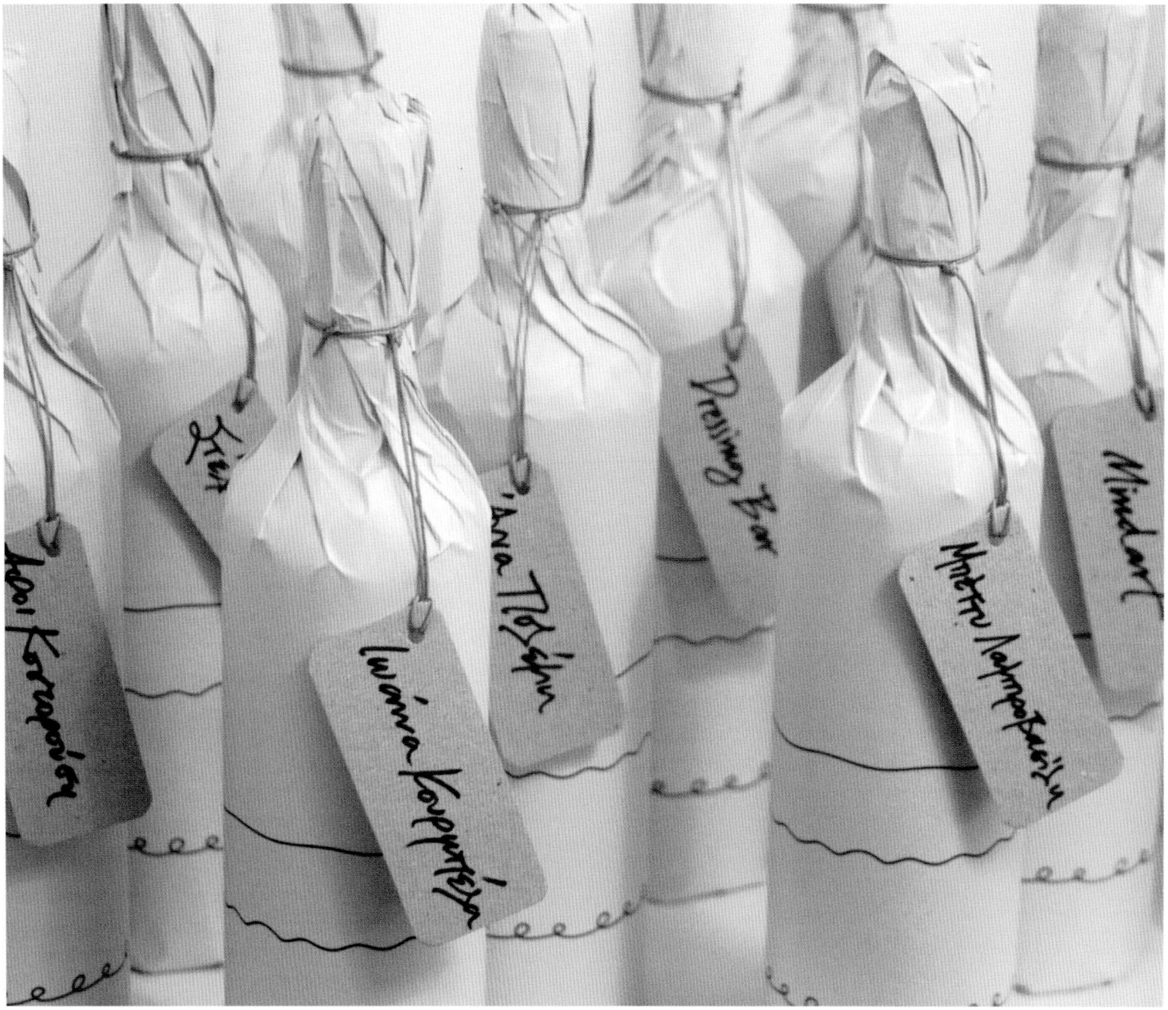

114/
ChrisTrivizas | Design • *The title 'Fygein adynaton' comes from the ancient Greek maxim 'Pepromenon phygein adynaton', meaning that fate cannot be avoided.*

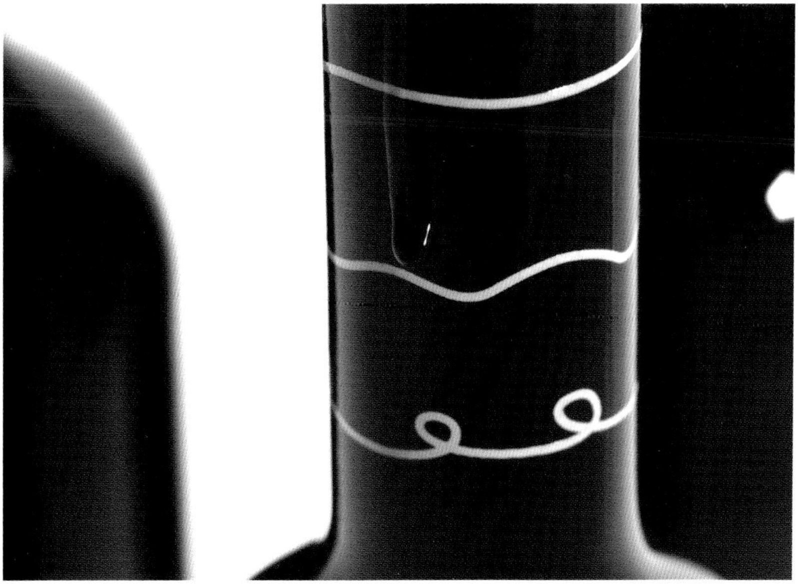

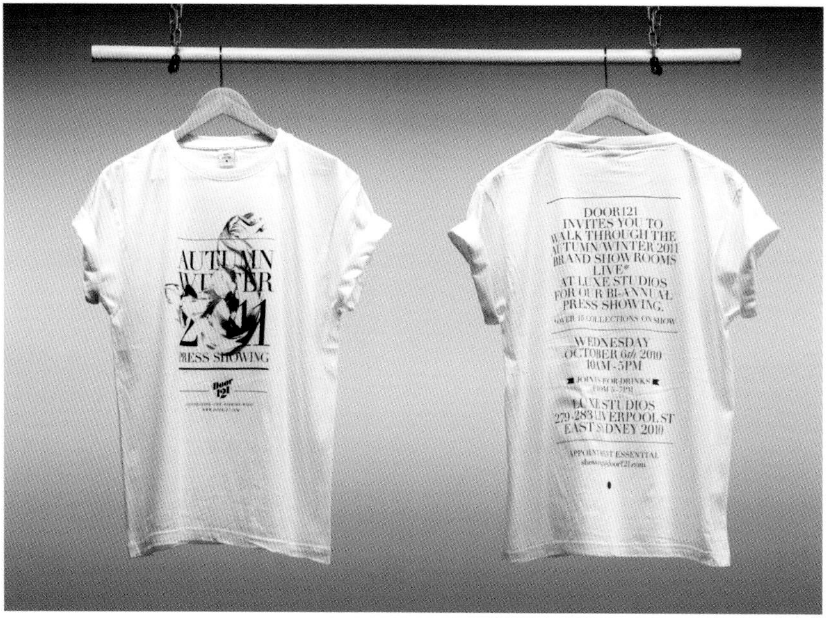

115/
Toben • *Door121 Autumn/Winter press showing invite. Hand-delivered to select media contacts.*

116/
Toben • *Give-away bag with Door121 key benefits printed on the inside.*

117/
Demetrio Mancini • *Some IKEA-style items for a minimal design store.*

118/
Make it Clear • *When Google and DoubleClick released their first product as a combined company, they were keen to let everyone know that the change was a good one. We showed that they were good on their own, but great together – like cheese and crackers.*

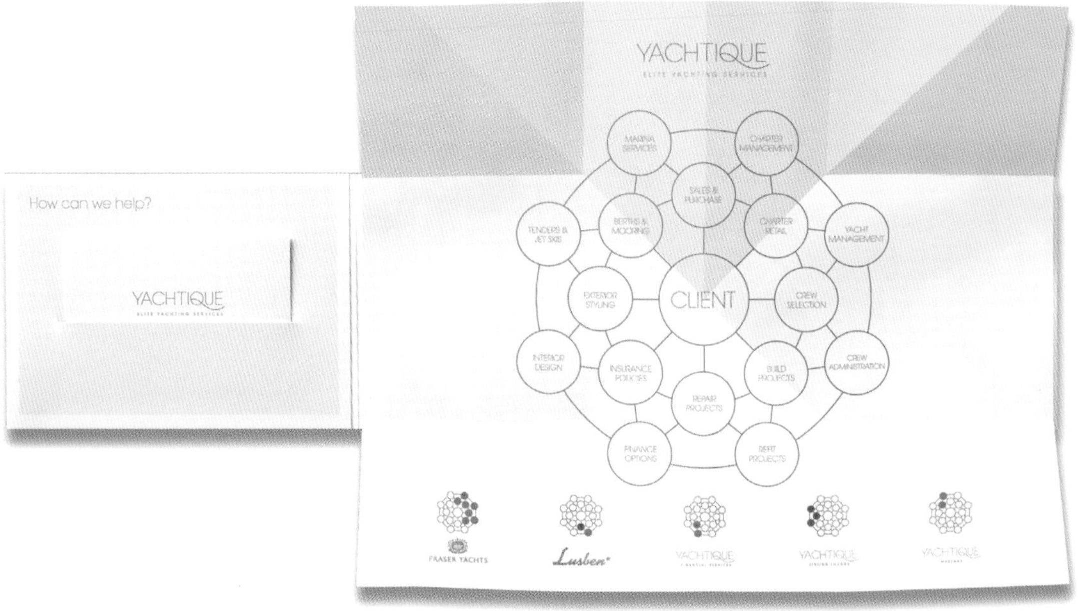

119/
SVIDesign • *This mailer, which promotes a new yachting services organization, is designed as a pop-up brochure with the company organization chart.*

120/
Hola Mimi • *Freelance project, self-managed by 47 illustrators from Argentina. Illustrators 2010 (10 cm x 15 cm format) has 47 postcards from 47 different Argentinian illustrators.*

121/
The Pencil Factory • *Promotional newsprint poster zine by the illustrators and designers in The Pencil Factory, Greenpoint, Brooklyn USA. Includes Kim Bost, Josh Cochran, Jennifer Daniel, Gilbert Ford, Jessica Hische, Grady McFerrin, Ted Mc Grath, Alex Eben Meyer, Chris Silas Neal, Zacharia O'Hora, Leif Parsons, Rachel Salomon, Joel Speasmaker, Jillian Tamaki, and Sam Weber.*

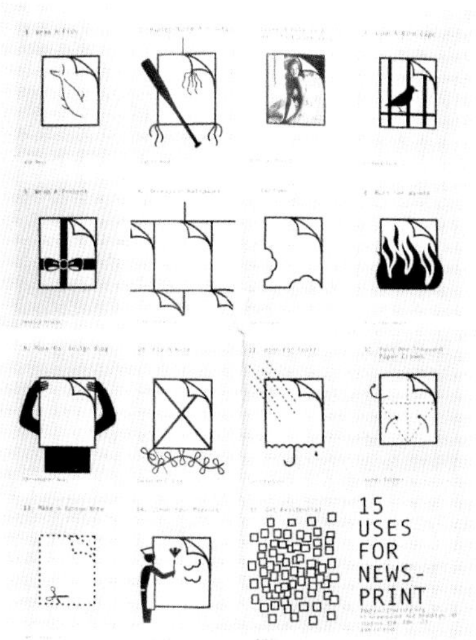
15
USES
FOR
NEWS-
PRINT

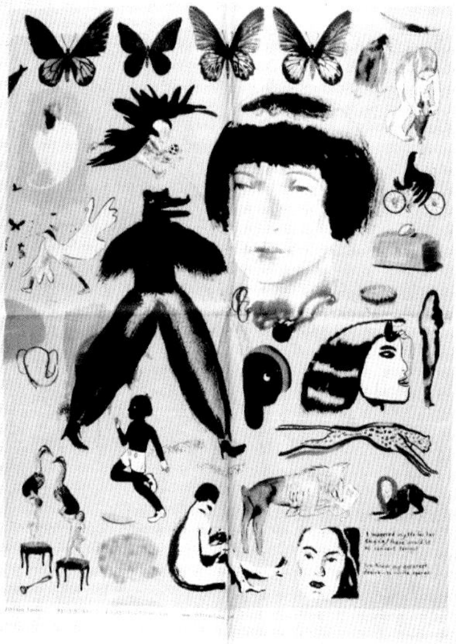

KATE
FINN
BEANS

122/
Versátil • *The 'Planet Earth Day' promotion campaign. The project includes the brand, the cleim, the graphic, video, etc.*

MEDIO
AMBIENTE
Y DESARROLLO
El sol no calienta igual para todo el mundo
Día de la Tierra, 22 de abril

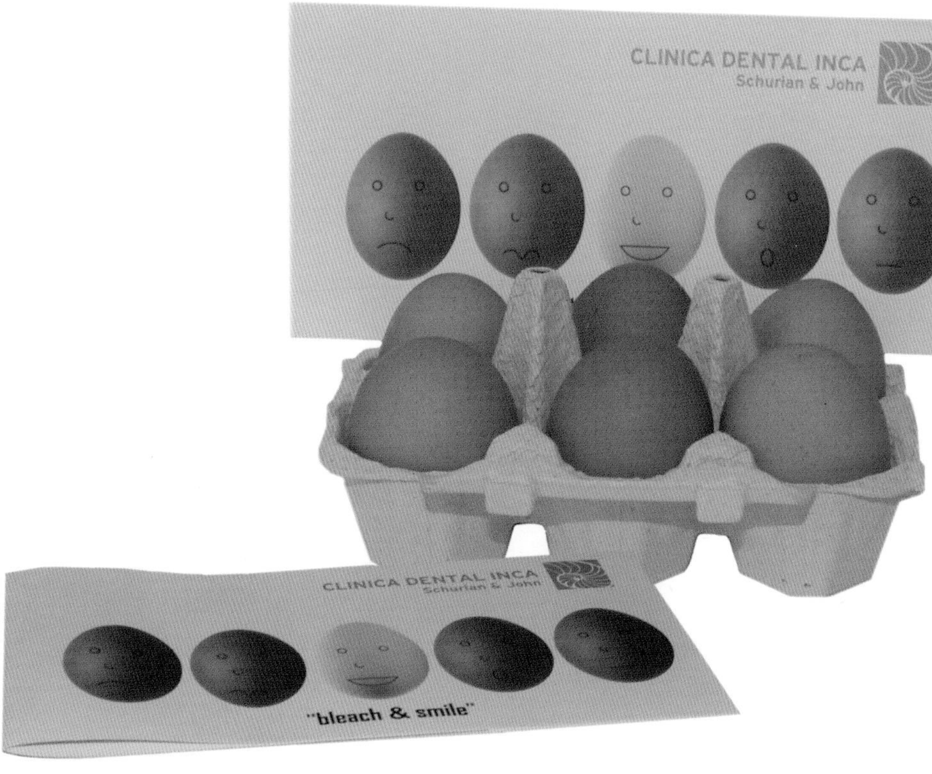

123/
VisioGlobal • *'Bleach & smile'. Promotional brochure for dental whitening.*

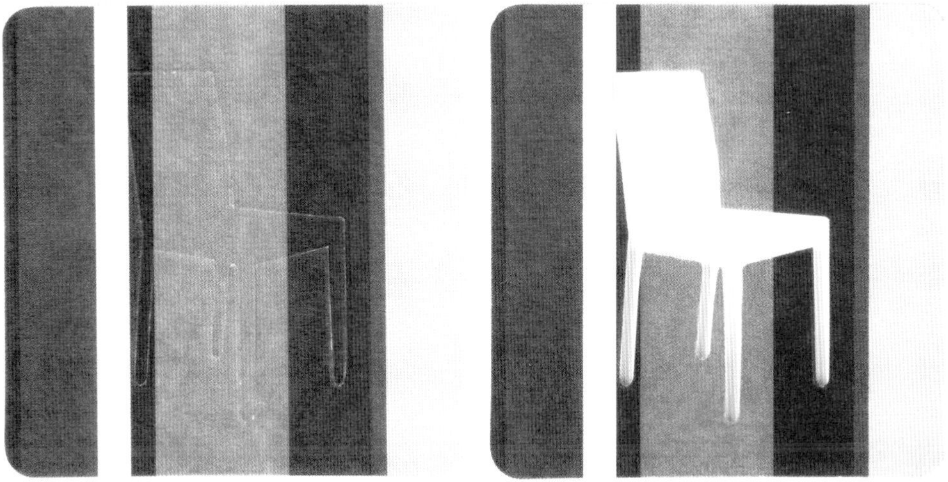

124/
Anna Pigem • *Coasters for an enterprise that sells chairs for hotels and restaurants.*

125/
estudio eckert+zúñiga • *Flaflaf's promotional booklet.*

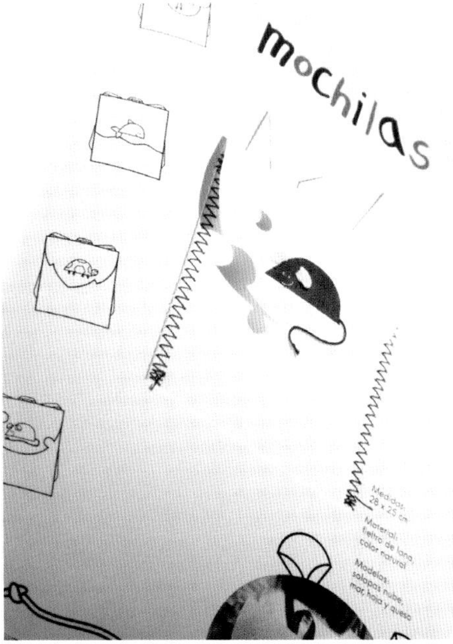
mochilas
Medidas: 28 x 25 cm
Material: fieltro de lana, color natural
Modelos: solapas nube, mar, hoja y queso

rjetas
nimadas para mandar
10,5 x 15 cm con sobre,
2 modelos.
flaflaf

flaflaf se llama
también esta exclusiva
colección de
camisetas, mochilas,
bufandas y gorras con
apliques en diferentes
telas y cordones.

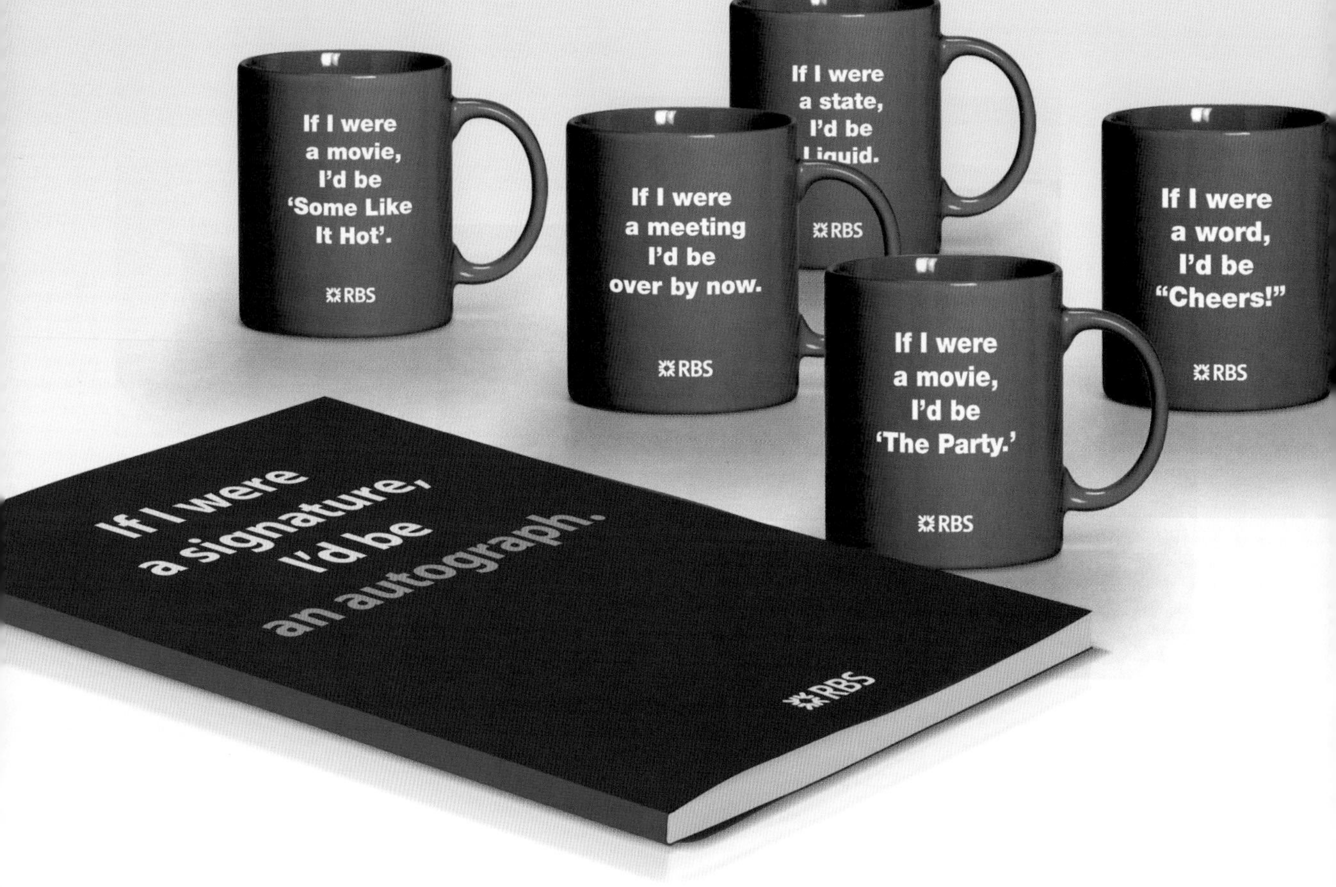

126/
Brandient • *Internal brand communication campaign, designed to convey RBS's brand idea: 'Finest quality banking'. Mugs and notepads were distributed.*

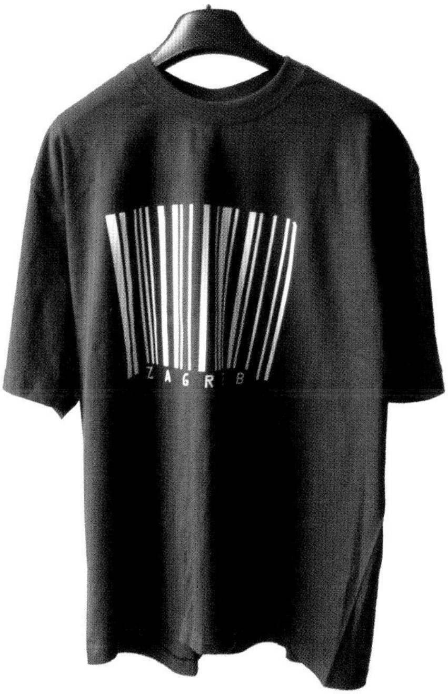

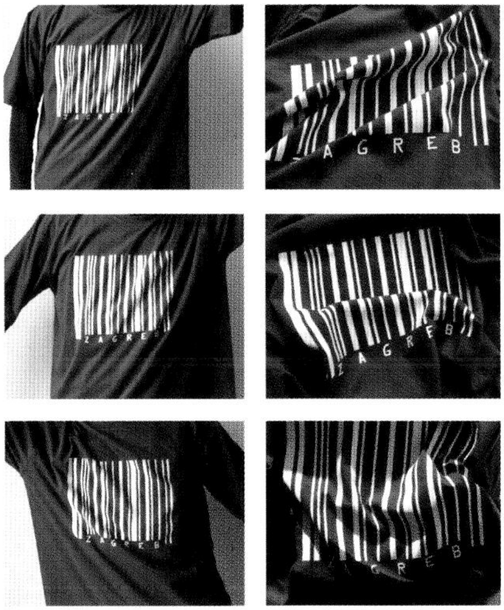

127/

Studio International • *The twentieth century has ended. A summary of its events, people, inventions... is under way. Bar code is a new typography for a new century.*

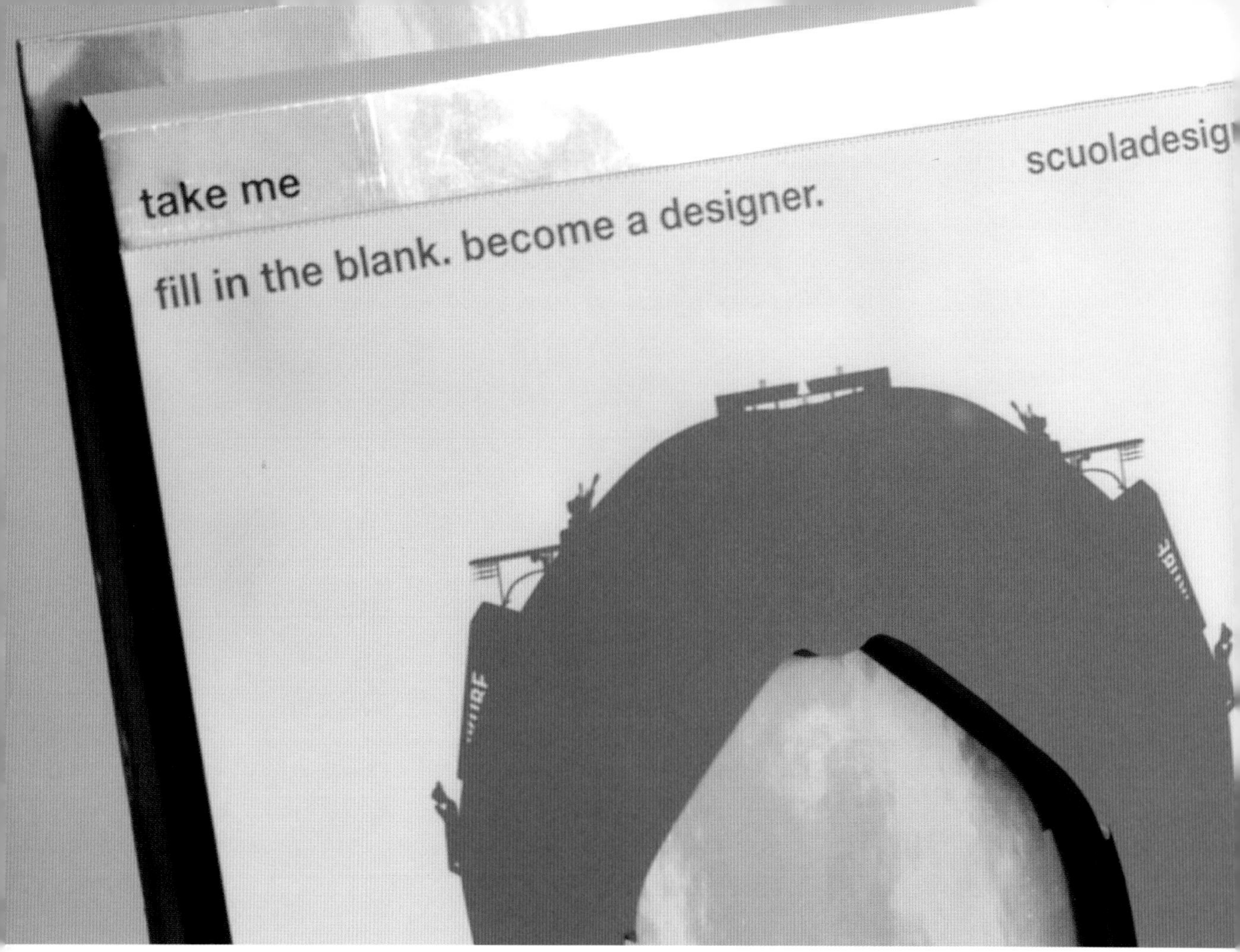

128/
jekyll & hyde • *On the occasion of the 'Salone del Mobile di Milano', we designed the promotional brochure for SPD, Scuola Politecnica di Design.*

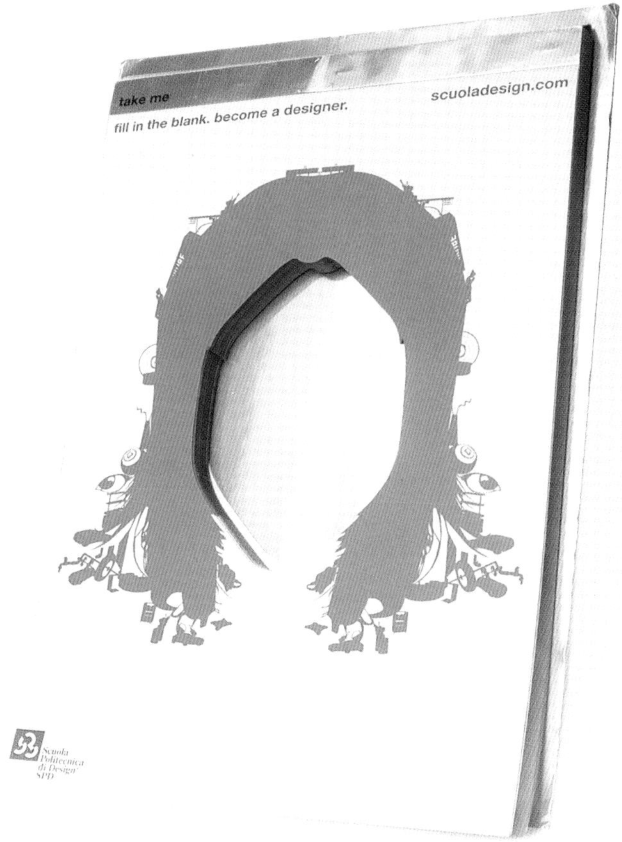
take me
scuoladesign.com
fill in the blank. become a designer.
Scuola
Politecnica
di Design
SPD

129/
housemouse • *'Wrapped by housemouse ™' is an award-winning designer wrapping paper range.*

130/
Albertini Romain • *Creation of hand-made 'anti crisis' business cards. All the stamped business cards are different and unique.*

131/
Studio International • *The logo MDC is made from two basic and diverse typographies with a visible and layered differentiating characteristic: the serif (De Vine) and grotesque (Helvetica).*

Muzejski

FSC
FEDRIGONI UK

132/
Design LSC • *A series of limited edition handbooks for designers and printers presenting Fedrigoni's Collection of FSC papers. Inspired by the many different textures and colours to be found within the range, each book uses die-cut coloured papers and illustrations to reference one of the classic elements: Earth, Water, Air and Fire.*

A Thanksgiving
Thanksgiving 2009
Thanksgiving 2009
Thanksgiving 2009
Sports Schedule
NBA
Orlando Magic @ Atlanta Hawks
TNT 8:00 PM EST
Chicago Bulls @ Utah Jazz
TNT 10:30 PM EST
NCAA Men's Basketball
Crunchy Apple Crisp
INGREDIENTS:
1 cup brown sugar
2 teaspoons ground cinnamon
1 unbeaten egg (very important)
DIRECTIONS:
Condiment Recipe
Cranberry Salsa
Yields - 3 cups
INGREDIENTS:
2 (15-ounce) cans pineapple tidbits
1 cup diced fresh cranberries
6 green onions, diced
1/2 cup diced dates
3 tablespoons honey
2 teaspoon lemon juice
2 1/2 teaspoons minced fresh ginger
1/2 teaspoon ground red pepper (optional)
DIRECTIONS:
Stir together first 7 ingredients and, if desired, pepper. Cover and chill at least 1 hour. Serve with ham or turkey.
Sports Schedule
NFL
Fox 12:30 PM EST
Oakland Raiders @ Dallas Cowboys
CBS 4:15 PM EST
New York Giants @ Denver Broncos
NFL Network 8:20 PM EST
NCAA Football
University of Texas @ Texas A&M
ESPN 8:00 PM EST
Tuskegee @ Alabama State
ESPNU 4:00 PM EST

We've enclosed eighteen place cards for your Thanksgiving table.
Write the name of each guest on the front of one of the cards and encourage them to write something they're thankful for on the back.
As you join together at the table for your Thanksgiving meal, invite each guest to share what they've written.

133/
Riverbed Design • *Together, Riverbed Design and Leatherback Printing offered a special gift for our clients that they could use during the holidays.*

MWM Graphics • *Glasses design, billboards, murals, print ads.*

135/
MWM Graphics • *Promotional deck of poker cards.*

Flou Flou - disoñadores asociados • *Cinquanta Cinquanta Skate Shop is based in Valencia. The image and the promotional elements have been created for them.*

137/
Raum Mannheim • *We designed icons for different types of promotional articles for the city of Mannheim, like shirts, bags, buttons, lanyards, cups, etc.*

L' ESPAI
L'E SPAI
L'ES PAI

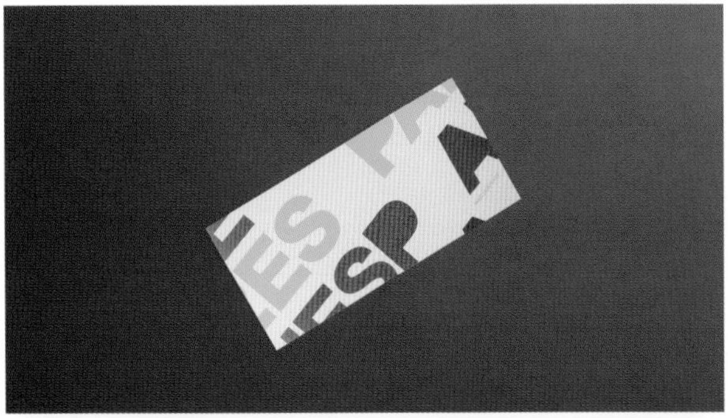

Bisgràfic • *'L'Espai': image of a youngsters' meeting space by using plates, adhesive tapes and other elements.*

139/
Edgar Bak • *FUTU DESIGN GUIDE magazine: promotional envelope.*

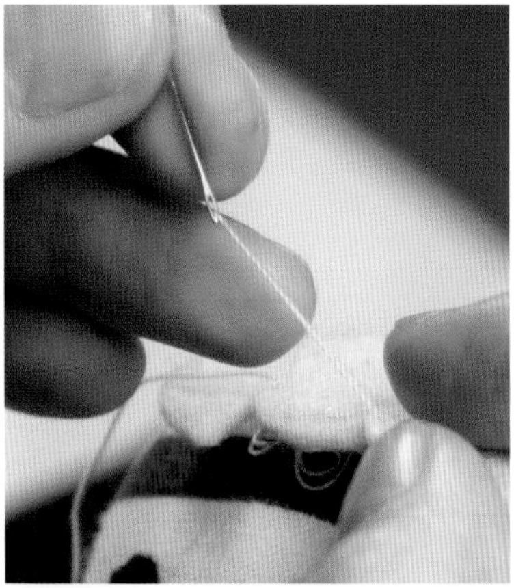

PixelBox Estudio Gráfico, S.L. • *Do-it-yourself package to make your own soft toy.*

141/
redondo design • *To promote the revitalization of CEG Gas Natural and CEG RIO offices in Brazil, we designed a special mug.*

142/

redondo design • *Redondo design created a fancy object made of the original product the company traded – stainless steel pipes. Redondo designed a vase that can be used such as a pencil holder or flower vase.*

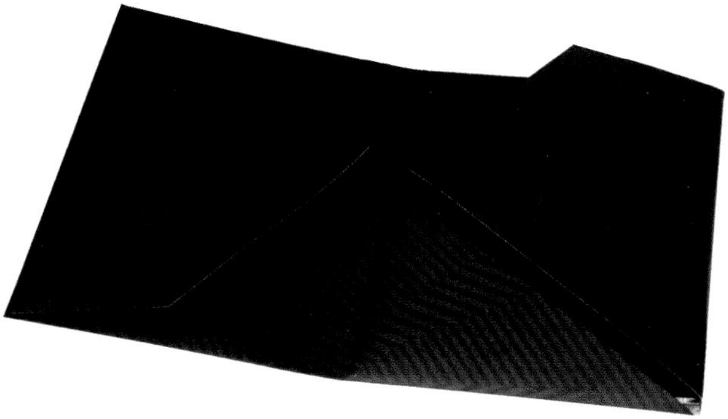

143/
Fluid • *Postcards promoting the agencies's work to be sent out to potential clients.*

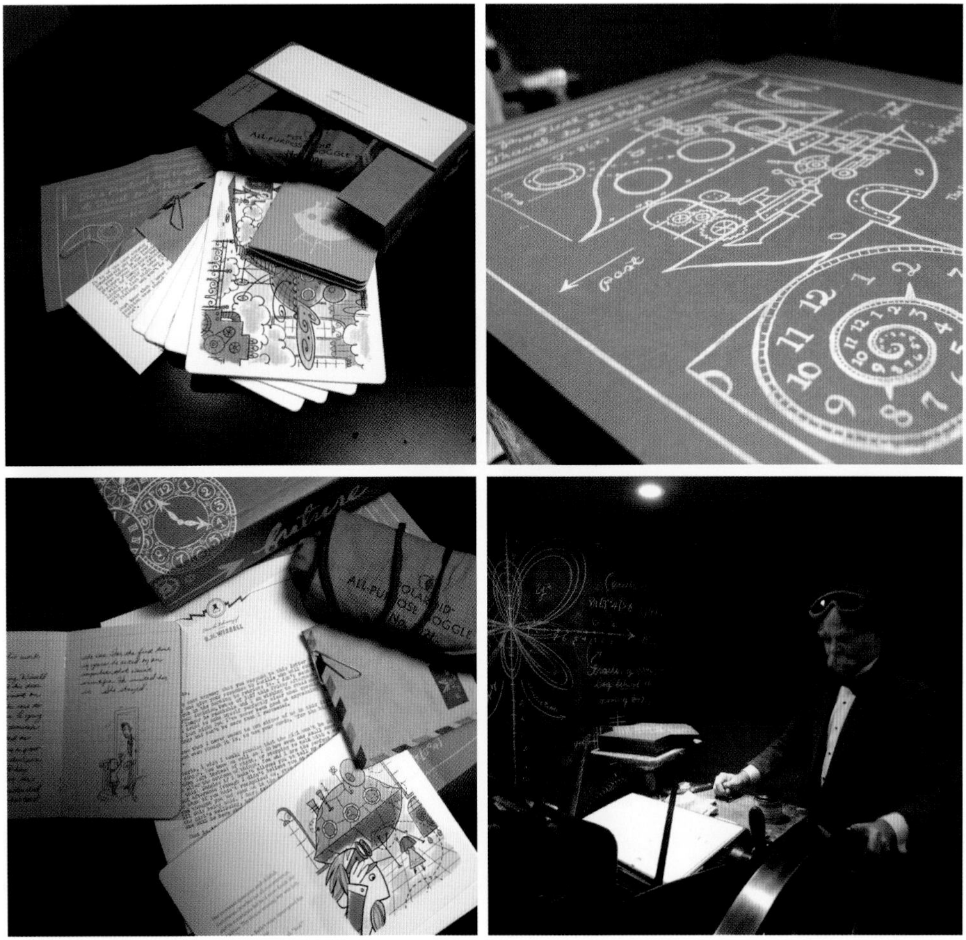

Belle & Wissell, Co. • *This limited-edition 'storykit' is an experiential collection of artifacts, artwork, and more that provide the backstory for the young Belle and her time-travel adventures.*

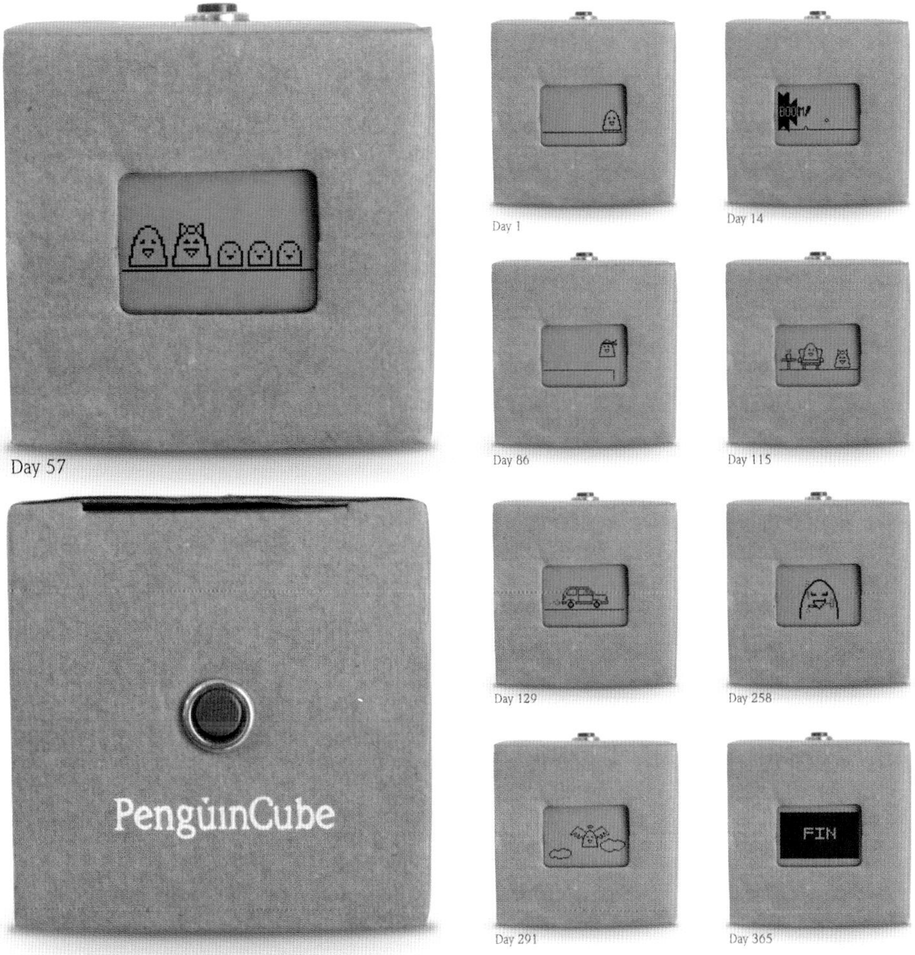

145/
PenguinCube • *PenguinCube is a design studio based in Lebanon. PiFive, a product of our annual PI (Promotional Item) tradition, is an animation in a box – viewable over the course of a year as a new frame gets unlocked every 12 hours.*

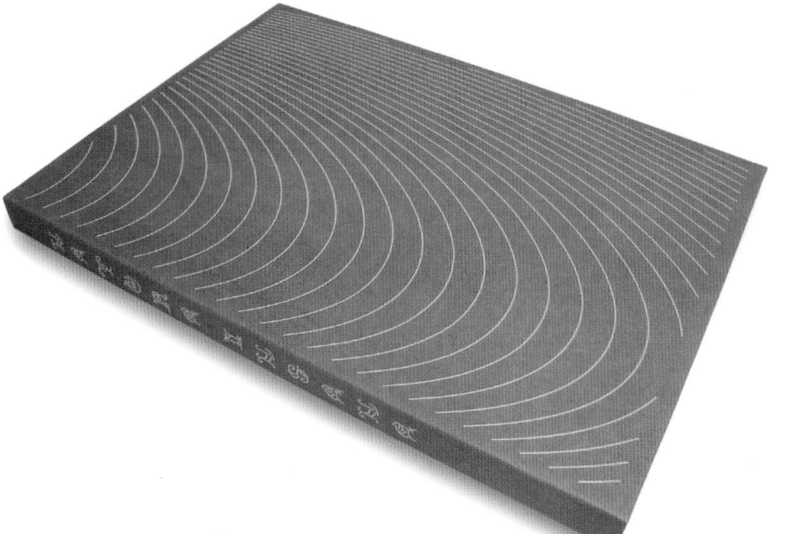

– mayke swarte – mark van wageningen – drukkerij bijlo –

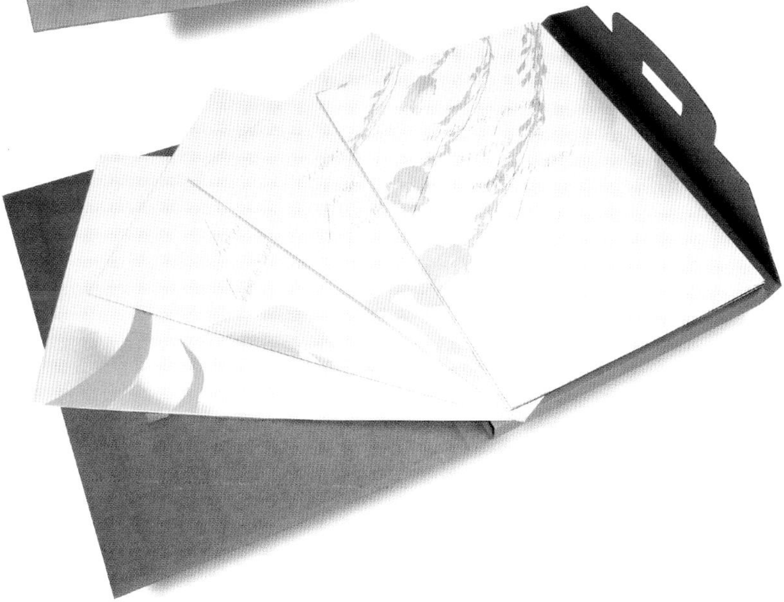

146/
Atelier van Wageningen • *Four folded posters (40 x 60 cm) in a small box are the calendar 'Natura Insana'. Not an easy-to-handle birthday calendar but pure beauty is the goal of this design.*

147/
Muro Buro • *A book of accumulated abandoned designs, which I recycled into a promotional direct mailer for Muro Buro.*

THE OWLS ARE NOT AS THEY SEEM!
I'M WORKING ON MY APPLE!
Hotel
MOTEL
Holiday Inn
All I want to do is ride my bike!
Take a leaf out of my book
Yeah! I'm going places
WILL DESIGN FOR FOOD!!
ON SECOND THOUGHT CASH WOULD BE MORE USEFUL!!

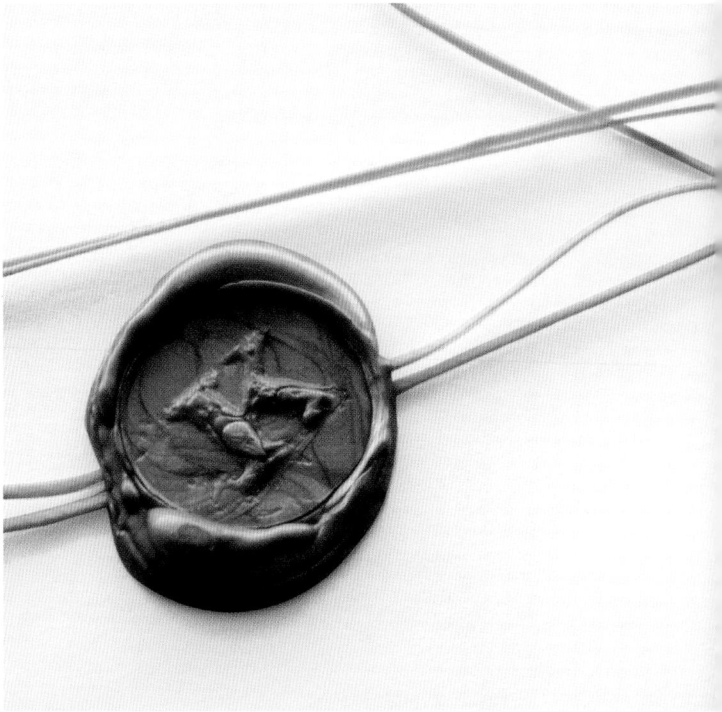

Kanella • *The main idea based on the story of Ariadne is to praise design by using a yellow thread. DESIGN is the KEY to the PATH towards the SUN.*

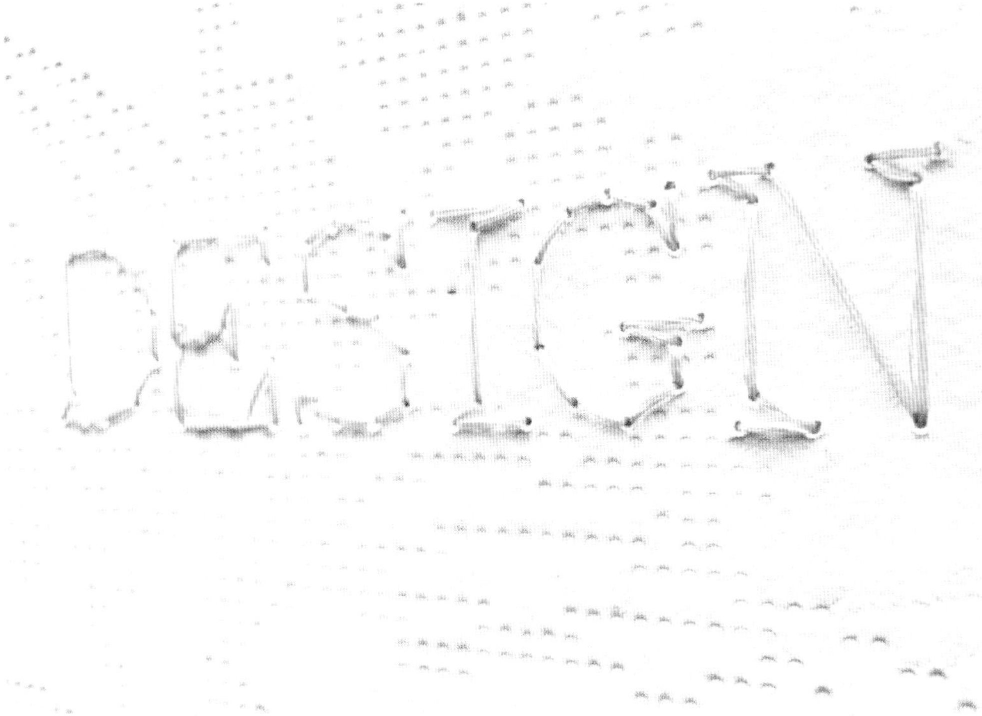
DESIGN

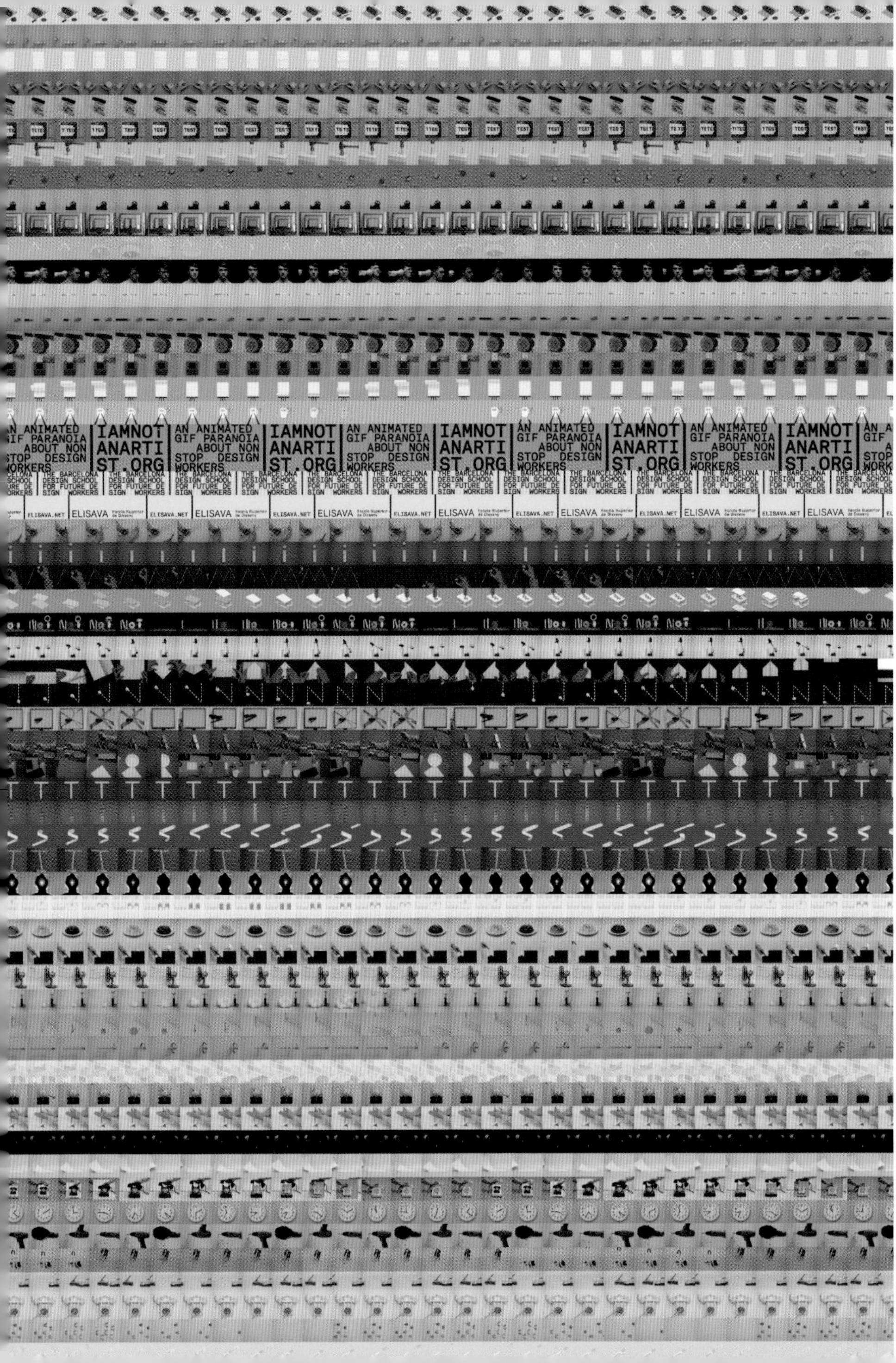
TEST
AN ANIMATED GIF PARANOIA ABOUT NON STOP DESIGN WORKERS
IAMNOT ANARTI ST.ORG
THE BARCELONA DESIGN SCHOOL FOR FUTURE DE SIGN WORKERS
ELISAVA.NET
ELISAVA

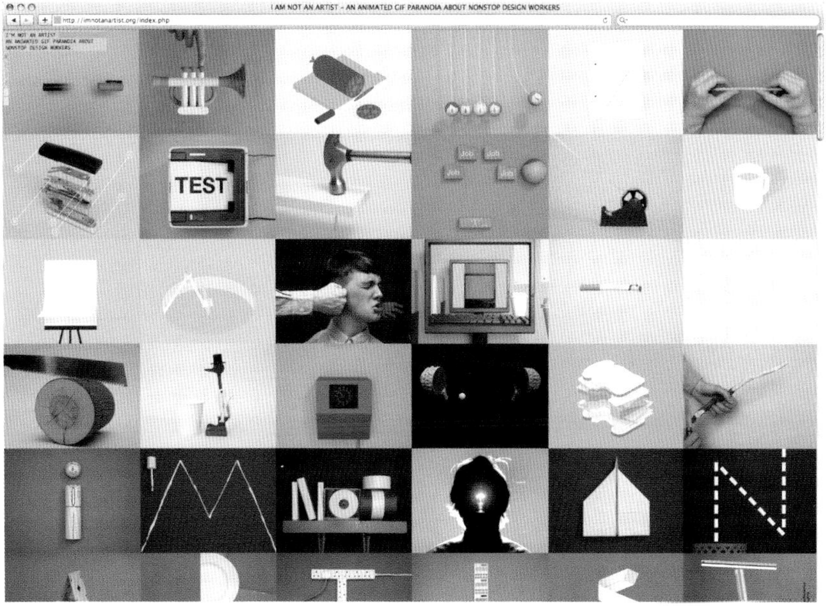

149/
Soon in Tokyo • *'I'am not an artist ' – an animated paranoia gif about non stop works. The project begins with 56 animated gifs.*

150/
Menta • *'DJ Taktel & Comodo's Control Remoto': design of the new record, poster and motion graphics. The best tribute that masters of sampler and the musical cut-n-paste could do for Saul Bass.*

DJ TAKTEL & COMODO's
CONTROL
REMOTO

151/
El Cuartel • *A bag for the 'MIMA', children's fair sponsored by Unicaja. Shows a girl swinging by the tree of the social work's values.*

152/
El Cuartel • *A mailing that contained pieces to build a little windmill with different types of paper.*

153/
Melville Brand Design • *Besides the ever changing fashion/articles, a wardrobe should contain a few must-have pieces. For Levi's these are the 'Levi's Essentials'.*

154/
José Bernabé Studio • *Corporate image program for a pet shop. In this specialized shop, you find personalized collars, beds, all kind of toys, fashion boutique and first quality food.*

155/
LLdesign • *Chiki is the eco-friendly wrapping cloth, originating from Japanese culture, where care for the environment and waste reduction are part of everyday life.*

NOTHING'S GONNA CHANGE MY WORLD
www.pixelbox.es

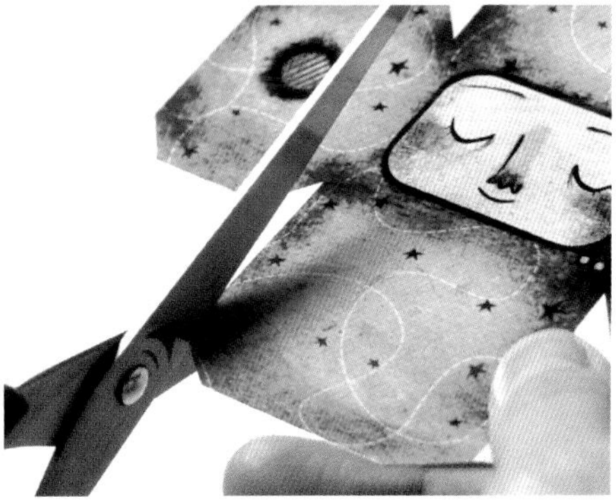

156/
PixelBox Estudio Gráfico, S.L. • *Cut out plate with robotín, our corporative character.*

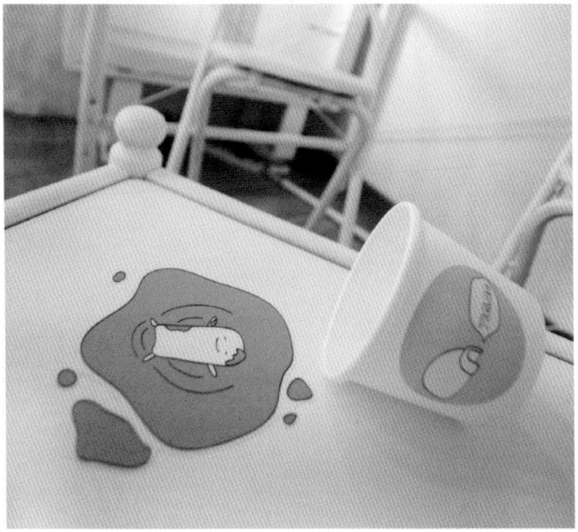

157/

Foreign Policy Design Group • *'Yigloo Yogurt' is all about fun and happiness. Whimsical and quirky characters were specially created for the brand and they were placed in unexpected corners and nooks in the store for customers to find or notice.*

PICK
A CUP

MIX
ANY FLAVOR

DRESS
ME UP

ENJOY
YUM!

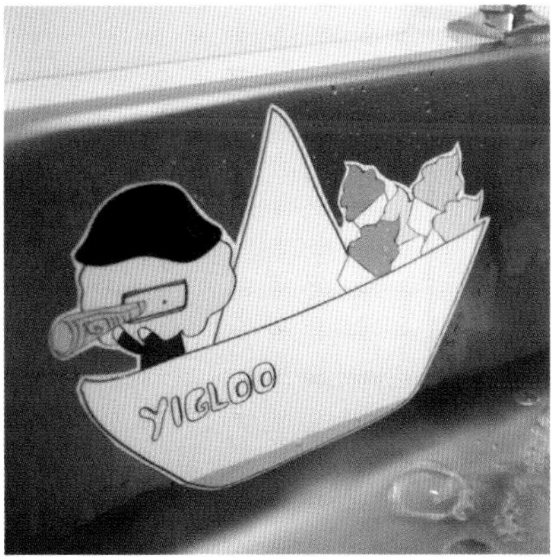

MOMO YOGGIE BONG TYLER

SHARE THE MOMENT
EUROVISION
SONG CONTEST
OSLO 2010
THE OFFICIAL PROGRAMME OF THE EUROVISION SONG CONTEST 2010

Handverk • *Eurovision Song Contest identity. Design of identity as well as a full range marketing campaign across all platforms.*

JCDecaux
HOLA

Bagasjeoppbevaring
Left baggage
Hittegods
Lost and found
Porter
Porter
SHARE THE
MOMENT

159/

UVE Diseño y Comunicación, S.L. • *Special packs to promote Nespresso's 12 major coffee flavors. Concept based on the claim 'The perfect cup of coffee for each time of day'. 12 different capsule-clocks are proposed for the brand's 12 main coffee varieties, which directly link 12 hours of the day, according to strength.*

160/
UVE Diseño y Comunicación, S.L. • *Press kit to promote the 'Nespresso Limited Crystal Collection' – a special edition of Nespresso machines featuring Swarovski's crystal incrustations.*

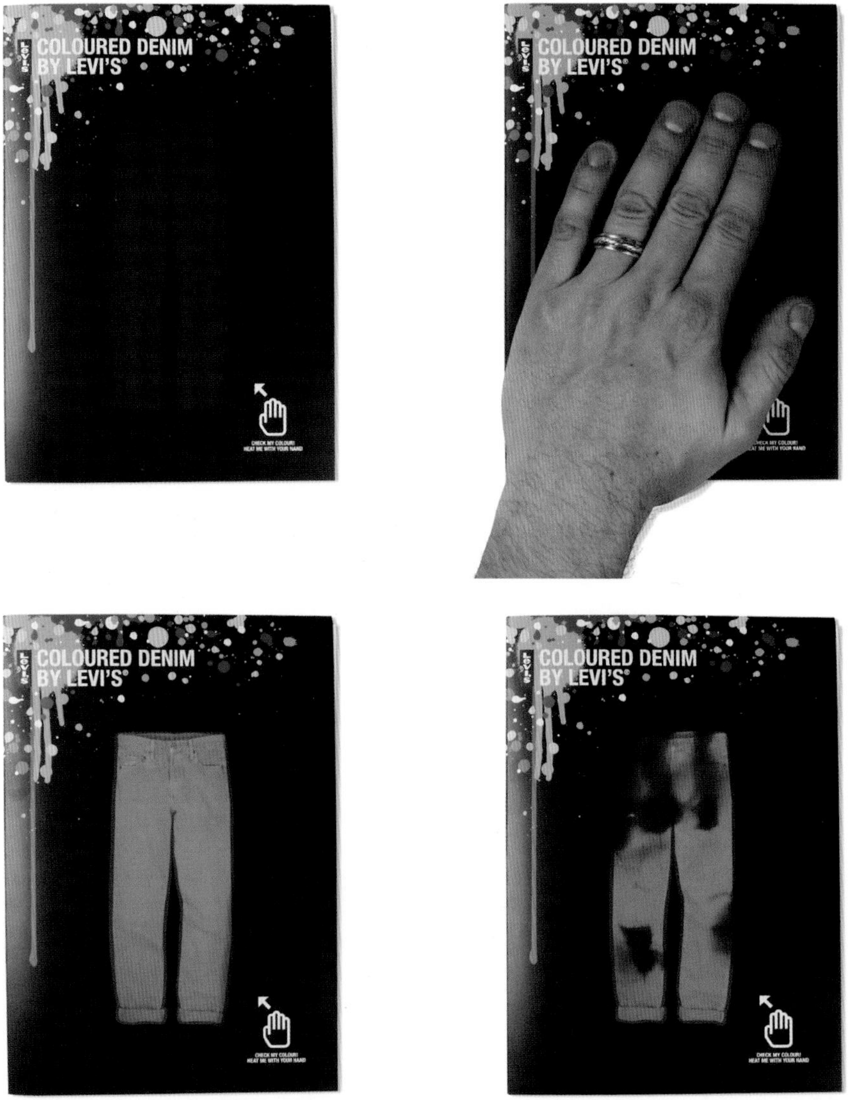

161/
Melville Brand Design • *'Check my color! Heat me with your hand' is the simple call to action on our latest mailing for Häberlein & Mauerer's, client Levi's.*

162/
Hola Mimi • *Illustration and calligraphy to apply on garments and accessories.*

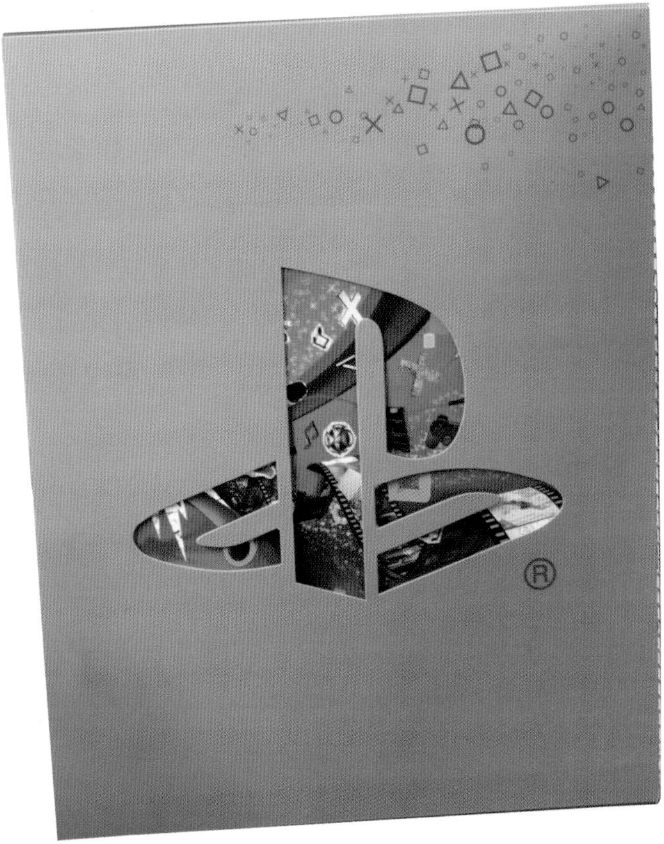

163/
Fluid • *Sony required an engaging brand book that packaged together all PLAYSTATION 3 and PSP (PlayStation Portable) and its titles and content into one pack.*

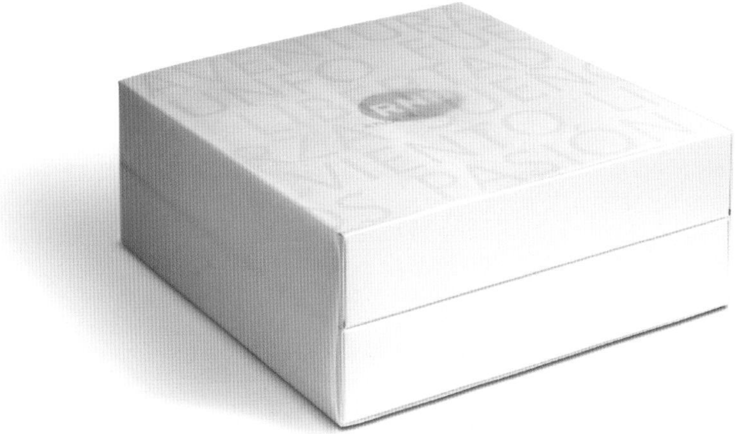

164/
Pepe Gimeno - Proyecto Gráfico • *RNB has made a special edition in miniature for COMOTÚ fragances and perfumes.*

165/
MWM Graphics • *Spring/Summer 2009 line: tee graphics.*

166/
Gorka Aizpurua Serrano • *Babysitter for your brand. Promotional campaign for the 'A Small Job' agency, an original and different way to generate visibility for brands.*

Descubra en el interior
una sorpresa bestial.

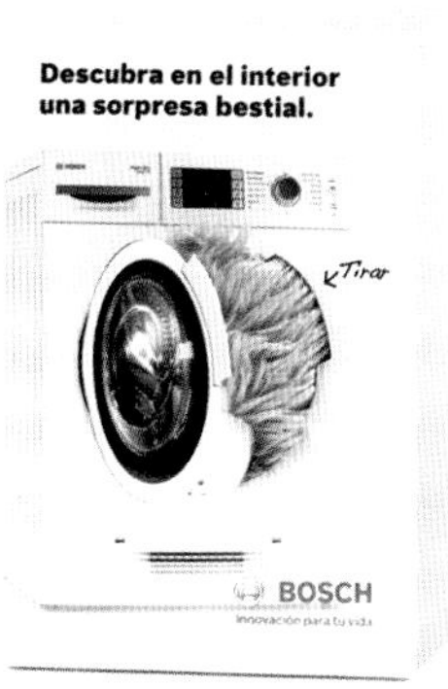

Descubra en el interior
una sorpresa bestial.

Esté muy atento porque a partir de ahora,
este león va a verse a todas horas...
... en todas las cadenas de TV...
Por fin
una lavadora
que además,
seca.
EL PAIS
... en los principales
periódicos nacionales...
... y también en internet.

167/
CUBO DISEÑO • *Bosch has presented their new washing-drying machine. Plv's were created for the selling point and a pack includes all the required informations.*

168/
Diseño Cdroig • *Pixels XL by Cdroig. New removable covering product.*

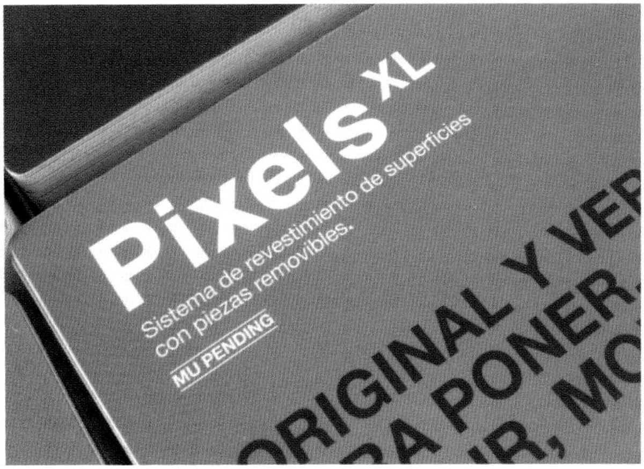
Pixels XL
Sistema de revestimiento de superficies
con piezas removibles.
MU PENDING
ORIGINAL Y
PONER,

I Pixels XL

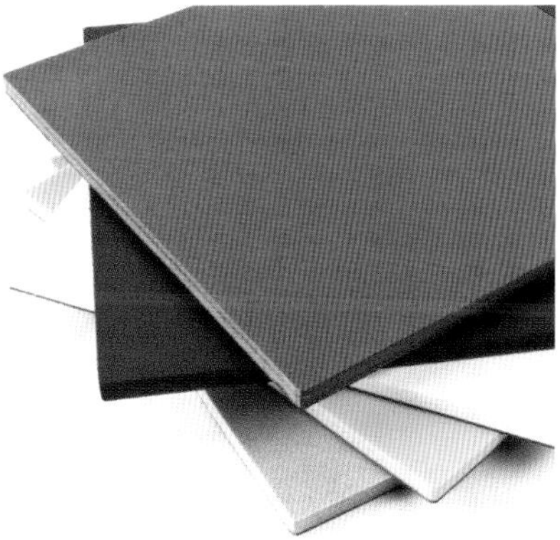

169/

JWT Brazil • *To launch the new formula of the flavors of Smirnoff Caipiroska, we created bottles with the texture of the fruit for the lemon, passion fruit and berry flavors, so that consumers could feel the unique experience of drinking a beverage made of fruit.*

DESCASQUE

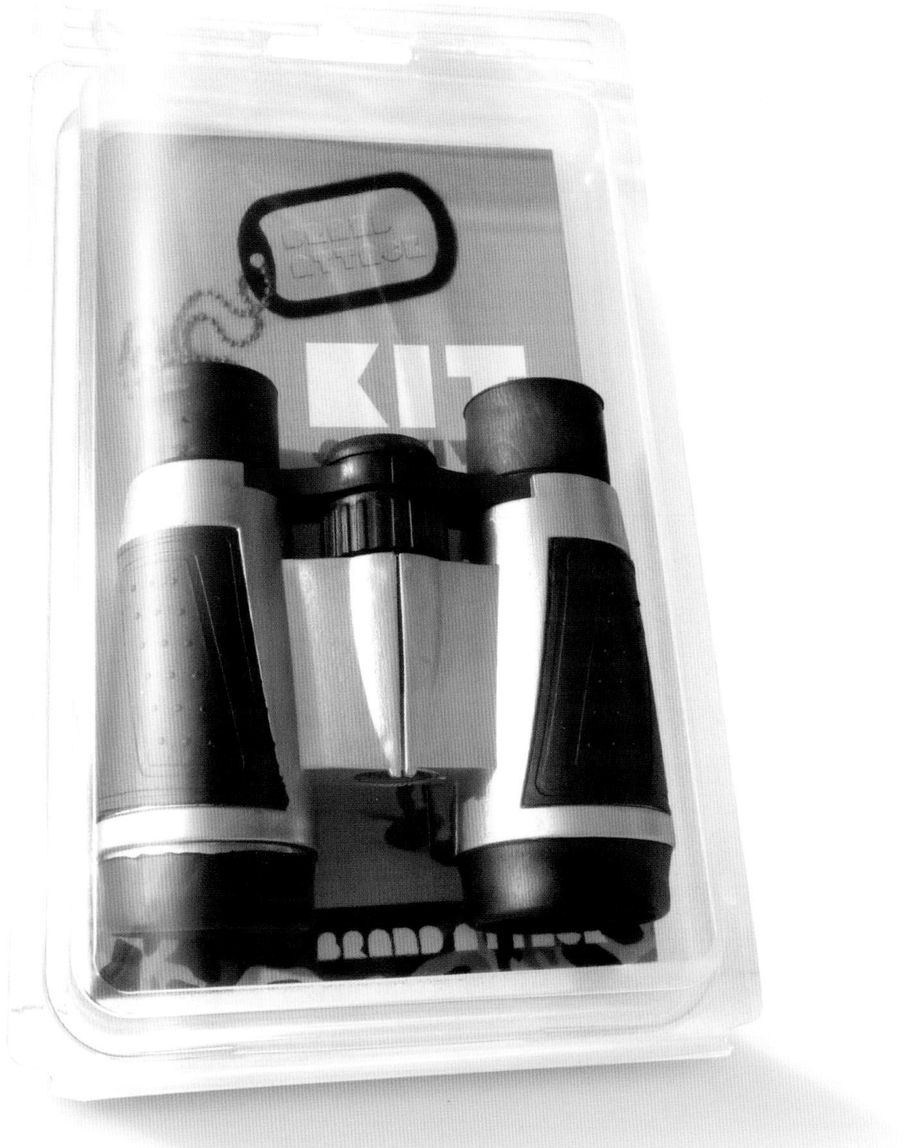

170/
Brand Attack • *KIT SURVIVAL. Promotional package for Brand Attack. Includes binoculars and map.*

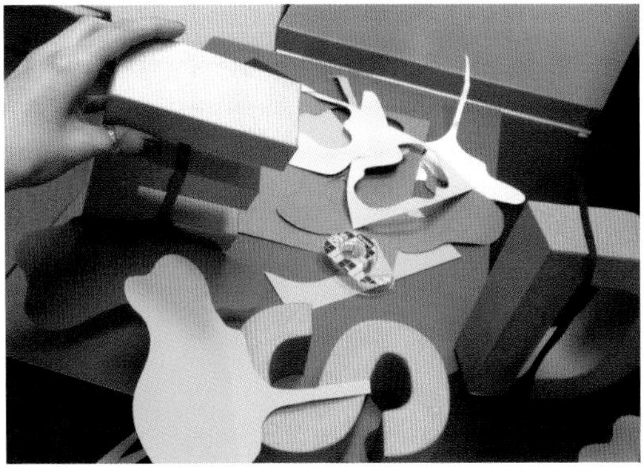

171/
María Luján • *Cardboard letters form the school name with a fountain of fine carboard.*

172/
Studio International • *Croatian tourism is based on sun and sea. This logo has two squares, red and blue, which represents also visual flag for the Republic of Croatia.*

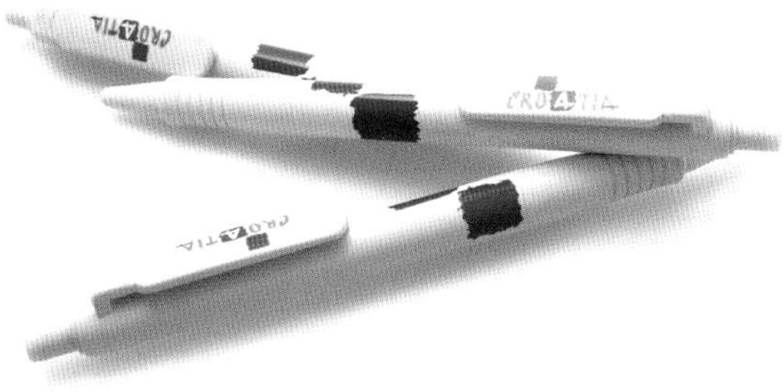

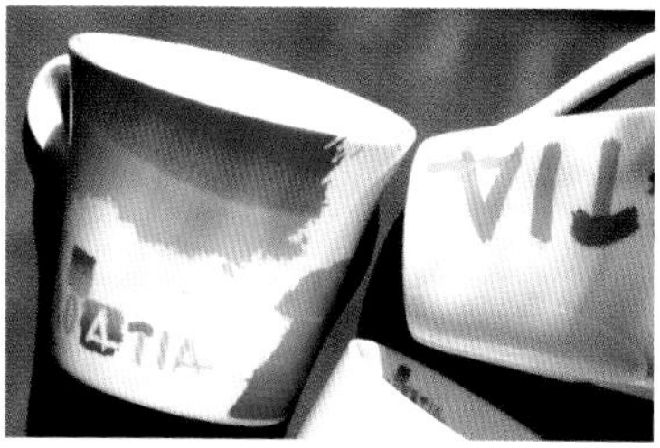

www.croatia.hr

173/
Bold°_a design company • *The idea was to draw attention to the launch of a new design firm creating a relevant and innovative way to promote it in both national and international markets.*

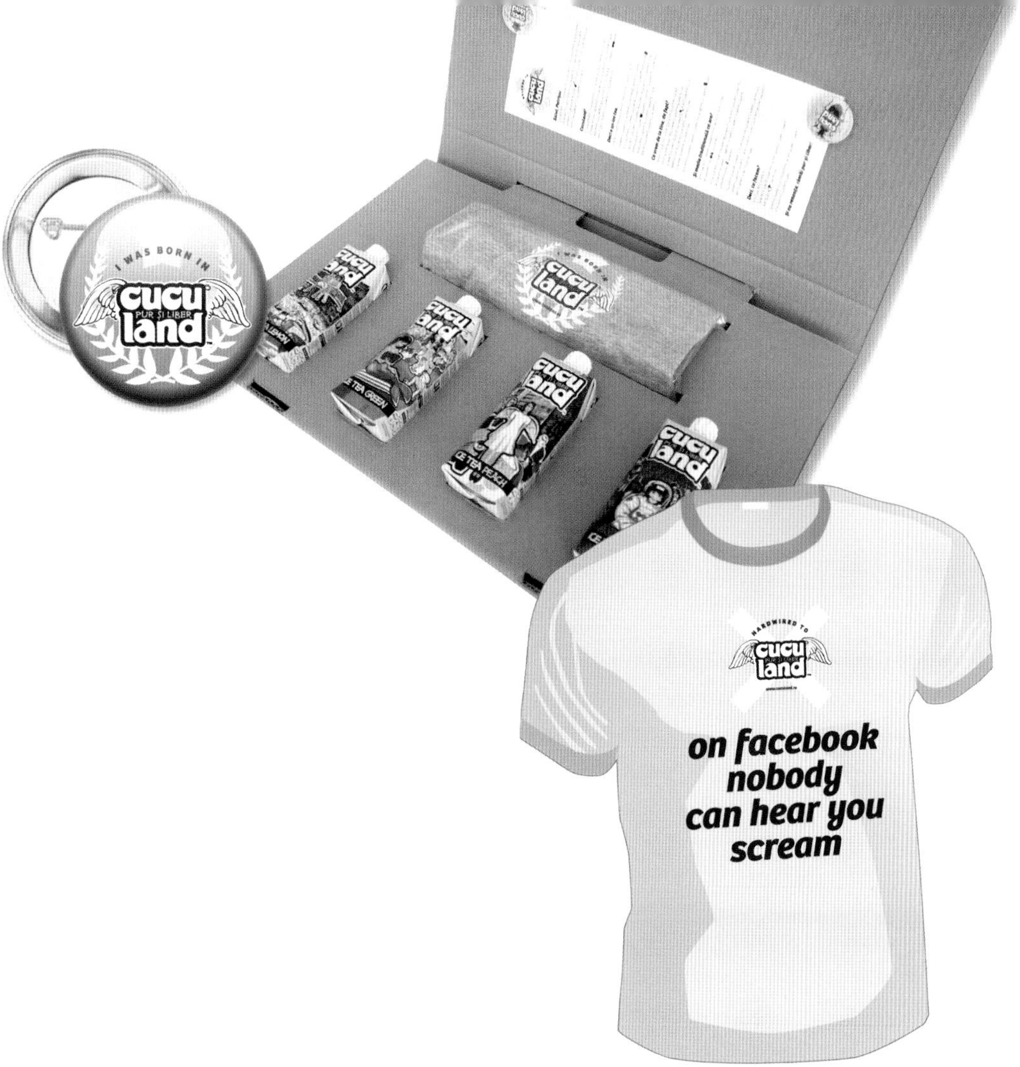

174/
Brandient • *Cuculand is a militant and cult brand inspired by the paradoxes and the everyday situations in contemporary Romania.*

L-WIZ FIGHT NO MORE FEATURING DON GOLIATH
ALL OUT DUBSTEP
STEREO
33 RPM
AOD001

175/
Ink Graphix • *Promotional record sleeves for the A'll Out Dubstep' vinyl releases, AOD001 and AOD003.*

NØRDIC MIST
BLACK IS BLACK
Artista invitado:
DJ CARLITO
Día:
SÁBADO 02 DE ENERO
Lugar / Hora:
ZONA NORDIC (DISCOTECA PLAYA CLUB) / 04:00H
Más Info:
WWW.MYSPACE.COM/ BLACKISBLACKMOTHERFUCKER
WWW.PLAYACLUB.NET

176/
David Silvosa | Arquitectura & Diseño • *Design for promotional flyers for funky music sessions.*

tangent°

tangent°

Hi.
We are
Tangent.
We
design.

TRUGBIL
design.
tangent°

Hi.
We are
Tangent.
We
design.
TRUGBIL
WINDING
tangent°

THE SPLITLIPPS
MOURN
FOR ROADKILL
DEBUT ALBUM OUT NOW
Hi.
We are
Tangent.
We
design.
Here are a few samples of our Orphan One label artwork - we just created the label to give you a taste of what we can do here at Tangent, our style and our way of thinking.
tangent
1 woodside terrace
glasgow g3 7uy
t +44 (0) 141 333 1785
e info@tangentgraphic.co.uk
w www.tangentgraphic.co.uk
TRUGBIL
WINDING
OUT 07/01/08
Druckenmiller

177/
Tangent Graphic • *We created a fictitious record label for which we designed albums. We then sent the designs on an A1 poster, housed in a record sleeve which we hand made, to record companies.*

178/
Fabien Barral • *To promote our 'Harmonie intérieure workshop', we designed a set of three letter-press coasters. (www.harmonie-interieure.com)*

SOCIÉTÉ D'HORTICULTURE ET DE VITICULTURE
CLERMONT-Fd
(Puy-de-Dome)
02
TOTAL
page 8
TÉLÉPHONE

BUREAU
DÉPARTEMENT
DU PUY-DE-DOME
COMMUNE
DU CONTRÔLEUR
No.
11 FEV
03167

Soon in Tokyo • *'Platos vs Platos' is a gastronomic-musical company. We propose good music and good food.*

Soon in Tokyo
presenta
italodisco
vs
La Mamma

1. Platos vs Platos ataca otra vez con **Italo Disco vs La Mamma**. **2.** Un menú inspirado en la vecchia cucina casera de la región de Véneto y en los recuerdos de infancia de nuestros chefs, acompañado por la banda sonora del macarra y futurista estilo surgido en los 80's. **3.** Los fogones están pilotados por los chefs del restaurante **Xemel** y la banda sonora, en manos de **Dave Bridge**. **4.** Los gemelos (en veneciano, xemei) Colombo, Max y Stéfano, junto a Mauri Devei, son los socios y embajadores de la cocina del Véneto en Barcelona. Ellos nos teletransportarán a la Venecia de los años 80, a sus grandes mesas familiares y sus recuerdos gastronómicos de las recetas de la Mamma. **5.** El periodista Dave Bridge (clubbingspain/scannerFM) se crió musicalmente con el italo-disco ochentero que de muy niño escuchaba en aquellas ferias de fiesta mayor de barrio. El género se convirtió en el hilo musical ideal para aquellos autos de choque que ahora ejercen de magdalena de Proust para nuestro disc jockey invitado. **6.** Este jueves, **16 de julio**, de **21:30h** a **1:00h**, en la calle Nápols nº 5. **7.** Menú degustación + bebidas = 65 euros por persona, todo incluido. **8.** Para esta ocasión, el aforo es limitado a 18 personas, todos sentados alrededor de nuestra mesa king size. **Entradas a la venta en platosvsplatos.com**
SOON IN TOKYO

Soon in Tokyo
presenta
TROPICALIA
vs
FRUTAORGIA

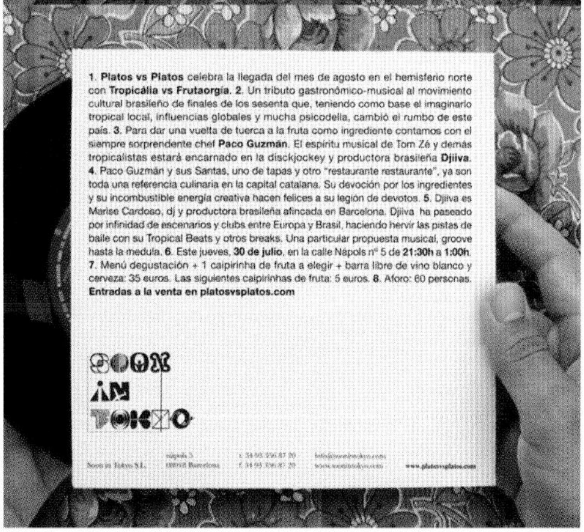
1. **Platos vs Platos** celebra la llegada del mes de agosto en el hemisferio norte con **Tropicália vs Frutaorgía**. **2**. Un tributo gastronómico-musical al movimiento cultural brasileño de finales de los sesenta que, teniendo como base el imaginario tropical local, influencias globales y mucha psicodelia, cambió el rumbo de este país. **3**. Para dar una vuelta de tuerca a la fruta como ingrediente contamos con el siempre sorprendente chef **Paco Guzmán**. El espíritu musical de Tom Zé y demás tropicalistas estará encarnado en la disckjockey y productora brasileña **Djiiva**. **4**. Paco Guzmán y sus Santas, uno de tapas y otro "restaurante restaurante", ya son toda una referencia culinaria en la capital catalana. Su devoción por los ingredientes y su incombustible energía creativa hacen felices a su legión de devotos. **5**. Djiiva es Marise Cardoso, dj y productora brasileña afincada en Barcelona. Djiiva ha paseado por infinidad de escenarios y clubs entre Europa y Brasil, haciendo hervir las pistas de baile con su Tropical Beats y otros breaks. Una particular propuesta musical, groove hasta la medula. **6**. Este jueves, **30 de julio**, en la calle Nápols nº 5 de **21:30h** a **1:00h**. **7**. Menú degustación + 1 caipirinha de fruta a elegir + barra libre de vino blanco y cerveza: 35 euros. Las siguientes caipirinhas de fruta: 5 euros. **8**. Aforo: 60 personas. **Entradas a la venta en platosvsplatos.com**
SOON IN TOKYO

concept, art-direction & design by Monique Kneepkens > www.monsworks
Florian Groehn > www.floriangroehn.com
retouching by Justin Overell > www.londesign.com.au
make-up by Lily Fontana > www.lilyfontana.com.au
models by Dallys Models > www.dallysmodels.com

180/
Monique Kneepkens • *This was a project I did as a self-promotional piece – to gain freelance work – and to do a nice folio piece. The idea, inspired by Valentine's Day, was to aim for the heart of those studios/agencies I love the most.*

001/ - Promo number
Albertini Romain - Studio name
Club Blister - Client name
France - Country

CLUB BLISTER is a London- and Paris-based collective of DJs, designers, musicians and promoters. - Promo description

107/
El Paso, Galería de Comunicación
Self-promotion
Spain

'We are our projects'. At El Paso we are our logos. With this philosophy, we design magnets to point out the nature of our work.

108/
VisioGlobal
Tomates Azules
Spain

For tastes, colours. Promotional element for 'Tomates azules'.

109/
ATIPUS
Self-promotion
Spain

To entertain your peaceful moments during the summer holidays, we recreated the mythic game 'Battleship', in two pocket notebooks; neither electricity nor Internet connections are required!

110/
Bisgràfic
Bryks
Spain

Promotional tee-shirts for Bryks, an on line brand for design's objects.

111/
Sandwich
Self-promotion
Spain

Sandwich's picnic. Corporate and promotional campaign.

112/
Virbia
IFR
Spain

Promotional mailing to capture the attention of new clients.

113/
Bunch
Consultants
Croatia

For two years in a row, we helped the Consultants real estate investors start the New Year with new collateral. In 2010 a screen-printed planner in an edition of 200 was produced along with a newly designed calendar and colorful range of Christmas cards.

114/
ChrisTrivizas | Design
Chris Trivizas
Greece

The title 'Fygein adynaton' comes from the ancient Greek maxim 'Pepromenon phygein adynaton', meaning that fate cannot be avoided.

115/
Toben
Door121
Australia

Door121 Autumn/Winter press showing invite. Hand-delivered to select media contacts.

116/
Toben
Door121
Australia

Give-away bag with Door121 key benefits printed on the inside.

117/
Demetrio Mancini
Civico
Italy

Some IKEA-style items for a minimal design store.

118/
Make it Clear
DoubleClick by Google
United Kingdom

When Google and DoubleClick released their first product as a combined company, they were keen to let everyone know that the change was a good one. We showed that they were good on their own, but great together – like cheese and crackers.

119/
SVIDesign
Yachtique, Italy
United Kingdom

This mailer, which promotes a new yachting services organization, is designed as a pop-up brochure with the company organization chart.

120/
Hola Mimi
47 Postales de Ilustradores Argentinos
Argentina

Freelance project, self-managed by 47 illustrators from Argentina. Illustrators 2010 (10 cm x 15 cm format) has 47 postcards from 47 different Argentinian illustrators.

121/
The Pencil Factory
The Pencil Factory
United States

Promotional newsprint poster zine by the illustrators and designers in The Pencil Factory, Greenpoint, Brooklyn USA. Includes Kim Bost, Josh Cochran, Jennifer Daniel, Gilbert Ford, Jessica Hische, Grady McFerrin, Ted Mc Grath, Alex Eben Meyer, Chris Silas Neal, Zacharia O'Hora, Leif Parsons, Rachel Salomon, Joel Speasmaker, Jillian Tamaki, and Sam Weber. Credits. Cover: Jennifer Daniel. Clockwise: Jennifer Daniel, Jillian Tamaki, Chris Silas Neal, Rachel Salomon.

122/
Versátil
Ingeniería sin fronteras
Spain

The 'Planet Earth Day' promotion campaign. The project includes the brand, the cleim, the graphic, video, etc.

123/
VisioGlobal
Zahnartzpraxis Schurian
Spain

'Bleach & smile'. Promotional brochure for dental whitening.

124/
Anna Pigem
Silleria Vergés
Spain

Coasters for an enterprise that sells chairs for hotels and restaurants. Photos: Estudi9dotze.

125/
estudio eckert+zúñiga
Flaflaf
Spain

Flaflaf's promotional booklet.

126/
Brandient
Royal Bank of Scotland
Romania

Internal brand communication campaign, designed to convey RBS's brand idea: 'Finest quality banking'. Mugs and notepads were distributed.

127/
Studio International
Zagreb City
Croatia

The twentieth century has ended. A summary of its events, people, inventions... is under way. Bar code is a new typography for a new century.

128/
jekyll & hyde
Scuola Politecnica di Design SPD
Italy

On the occasion of the 'Salone del Mobile di Milano', we designed the promotional brochure for SPD, Scuola Politecnica di Design.

129/
housemouse
housemouse
Australia

'Wrapped by housemouse™' is an award-winning designer wrapping paper range.

130/
Albertini Romain
Self-promotion
France

Creation of hand-made 'anti crisis' business cards. All the stamped business cards are different and unique.

131/
Studio International
Museum Documentation Centre
Croatia

The logo MDC is made from two basic and diverse typographies with a visible and layered differentiating characteristic: the serif (De Vine) and grotesque (Helvetica).

132/
Design LSC
Fedrigoni
United Kingdom

A series of limited edition handbooks for designers and printers presenting Fedrigoni's Collection of FSC papers. Inspired by the many different textures and colours to be found within the range, each book uses die-cut coloured papers and illustrations to reference one of the classic elements: Earth, Water, Air and Fire.

133/
Riverbed Design
Leatherback Printing
United States

Together, Riverbed Design and Leatherback Printing offered a special gift for our clients that they could use during the holidays.

134/
MWM Graphics
RAY BAN
United States

Glasses design, billboards, murals, print ads.

135/
MWM Graphics
D MAGIC TRICKS
United States

Promotional deck of poker cards.

136/
Flou Flou - disoñadores asociados
CinquantaCinquanta Skate Shop
Spain

Cinquanta Cinquanta Skate Shop is based in Valencia. The image and the promotional elements have been created for them.

137/
Raum Mannheim
Stadt Mannheim
Germany
We designed icons for different types of promotional articles for the city of Mannheim, like shirts, bags, buttons, lanyards, cups, etc.

138/
Bisgràfic
Ajuntament de Roda
Spain

'L'Espai': image of a youngsters' meeting space by using plates, adhesive tapes and other elements.

139/
Edgar Bak
Publishing and Design Group
Poland

FUTU DESIGN GUIDE magazine: promotional envelope.

140/
PixelBox Estudio Gráfico S.L.
Ciudad Tecnológica Valnalón
Spain

Do-it-yourself package to make your own soft toy.

141/
redondo design
CEG GasNatural CEG RIO
Brazil

To promote the revitalization of CEG Gas Natural and CEG RIO offices in Brazil, we designed a special mug.

142/
redondo design
InoxTubos
Brazil

Redondo design created a fancy object made of the original product the company traded – stainless steel pipes. Redondo designed a vase that can be used such as a pencil holder or flower vase.

143/
Fluid
Fluid
United Kingdom

Postcards promoting the agencies's work to be sent out to potential clients.

144/
Belle & Wissell, Co.
Self-promotion
United States

This limited-edition 'storykit' is an experiential collection of artifacts, artwork, and more that provide the backstory for the young Belle and her time-travel adventures.

145/
PenguinCube
PenguinCube
Lebanon

PenguinCube is a design studio based in Lebanon. PiFive, a product of our annual PI (Promotional Item) tradition, is an animation in a box – viewable over the course of a year as a new frame gets unlocked every 12 hours.

146/
Atelier van Wageningen
Self-promotion
Netherlands

Four folded posters (40 x 60 cm) in a small box are the calendar 'Natura Insana'. Not an easy-to-handle birthday calendar but pure beauty is the goal of this design.

147/
Muro Buro
Self-promotion
United Kingdom

A book of accumulated abandoned designs, which I recycled into a promotional direct mailer for Muro Buro.

148/
Kanella
Kanella
Greece

The main idea based on the story of Ariadne is to praise design by using a yellow thread. DESIGN is the KEY to the PATH towards the SUN.

149/
Soon in Tokyo
Elisava
Spain

'I'am not an artist' – an animated paranoia gif about non stop works. The project begins with 56 animated gifs.

150/
Menta
Coffy records
Spain

'DJ Taktel & Comodo's Control Remoto': Design of the new record, poster and motion graphics. The best tribute that masters of sampler and the musical cut-n-paste could do for Saul Bass.

151/
El Cuartel
Obra Social Unicaja
Spain

A bag for the 'MIMA', children's fair sponsored by Unicaja. Shows a girl swinging by the tree of the social work's values.

152/
El Cuartel
Artigraf
Spain

A mailing that contained pieces to build a little windmill with different types of paper.

153/
Melville Brand Design
Levi's
Germany

Besides the ever changing fashion/ articles, a wardrobe should contain a few must-have pieces. For Levi's these are the 'Levi's Essentials'.

154/
José Bernabé Studio
D&C
Spain

Corporate image program for a pet shop. In this specialized shop, you find personalized collars, beds, all kind of toys, fashion boutique and first quality food.

155/
LLdesign
il paradiso dei calzini
Italy

Chiki is the eco-friendly wrapping cloth, originating from Japanese culture, where care for the environment and waste reduction are part of everyday life.

156/
PixelBox Estudio Gráfico S.L
Self-promotion
Spain

Cut out plate with robotín, our corporative character.

157/
Foreign Policy Design Group
Yigloo, Singapore
Singapore

'Yigloo Yogurt' is all about fun and happiness. Whimsical and quirky characters were specially created for the brand and they were placed in unexpected corners and nooks in the store for customers to find or notice.

158/
Handverk
European Broadcasting Union
Norway

Eurovision Song Contest identity. Design of identity as well as a full range marketing campaign across all platforms.

159/
UVE Diseño y Comunicación, S.L.
Nespresso
Spain

Special packs to promote Nespresso's 12 major coffee flavors. Concept based on the claim 'The perfect cup of coffee for each time of day'. 12 different capsule-clocks are proposed for the brand's 12 main coffee varieties, which directly link 12 hours of the day, according to strength.

160/
UVE Diseño y Comunicación, S.L.
Nespresso
Spain

Press kit to promote the 'Nespresso Limited Crystal Collection' – a special edition of Nespresso machines featuring Swarovski's crystal incrustations.

161/
Melville Brand Design
Levi's
Germany

'Check my color! Heat me with your hand' is the simple call to action on our latest mailing for Häberlein & Mauerer's, client Levi's.

162/
Hola Mimi
Chibel
Argentina
Illustration and calligraphy to apply on garments and accessories.

163/
Fluid
Sony Computer Entertainment Europe
United Kingdom

Sony required an engaging brand book that packaged together all PLAYSTATION 3 and PSP (PlayStation Portable) and its titles and content into one pack.

164/
Pepe Gimeno - Proyecto Gráfico
RNB
Spain

RNB has made a special edition in miniature for COMOTÚ fragances and perfumes.

165/
MWM Graphics
GLYPH CUE CLOTHING
United States

Spring/Summer 2009 line: tee graphics.

166/
Gorka Aizpurua Serrano
Juan Pablo Sanchez, "A Small Job"
Spain

Babysitter for your brand. Promotional campaign for the 'A Small Job' agency, an original and different way to generate visibility for brands.

167/
CUBO DISEÑO
Bosch
Spain

Bosch has presented their new washing-drying machine. Plv's were created for the selling point and a pack includes all the required informations.

168/
Diseño Cdroig
Self-promotion
Spain

'Pixels XL' by Cdroig. New removable covering product.

169/
JWT Brazil
Diageo
Brazil

To launch the new formula of the flavors of Smirnoff Caipiroska, we created bottles with the texture of the fruit for the lemon, passion fruit and berry flavors, so that consumers could feel the unique experience of drinking a beverage made of fruit.

170/
Brand Attack
Self-promotion
Spain

KIT SURVIVAL. Promotional package for Brand Attack. Includes binoculars and map.

171/
María Luján
ESDIP Escuela Superior de Dibujo Profesional
Spain

Cardboard letters form the school name with a fountain of fine carboard.

172/
Studio International
Croatian National Tourist Board
Croatia

Croatian tourism is based on sun and sea. This logo has two squares, red and blue, which represents also visual flag for the Republic of Croatia.

173/
Bold°_a design company
Self-promotion
Brazil

The idea was to draw attention to the launch of a new design firm creating a relevant and innovative way to promote it in both national and international markets.

174/
Brandient
Trigento Marketing
Romania

Cuculand is a militant and cult brand inspired by the paradoxes and the everyday situations in contemporary Romania.

175/
Ink Graphix
All Out Dubstep
Sweden

Promotional record sleeves for the 'All Out Dubstep' vinyl releases, AOD001 and AOD003.

176/
David Silvosa | Arquitectura & Diseño
Complejo Playa Club Coruña
Spain

Design for promotional flyers for funky music sessions.

177/
Tangent Graphic
Self-promotional
United Kingdom

We created a fictitious record label for which we designed albums. We then sent the designs on an A1 poster, housed in a record sleeve which we hand made, to record companies.

178/
Fabien Barral
Harmonie intérieure
France

To promote our 'Harmonie intérieure workshop', we designed a set of three letter-press coasters. (www.harmonie-interieure.com)

179/
Soon in Tokyo
Soon in Tokyo
Spain

'Platos vs Platos' is a gastronomic-musical company. We propose good music and good food.

180/
Monique Kneepkens
Self-promotion
Australia

This was a project I did as a self-promotional piece – to gain freelance work – and to do a nice folio piece. The idea, inspired by Valentine's Day, was to aim for the heart of those studios/agencies I love the most.

Final Directory

304 - 309

&Larry - studio name
013/ 081/ - promo number
www.andlarry.com - studio website

&Larry
013/ 081/
www.andlarry.com

Albertini Romain
001/ 130/
romainalbertini.fr

Aloof
054/
www.aloofdesign.com

Anna Pigem
018/ 124/
www.annapigem.com

Atelier van Wageningen
146/
www.ateliervanwageningen.nl

ATIPUS
009/ 027/ 109
www.atipus.com

Belle & Wissell, Co.
144/
www.bwco.info

Bisgràfic
110/ 138/
bisgrafic.com

Bold°_a design company
173/
www.bolddesign.com.br

Brand Attack
170/
www.brandattack.net

Brandient
126/ 174/
www.brandient.com

Bruno Baeza
032/
brunobaeza.com

Bunch
012/ 113/
www.bunchdesign.com

Carlitos y Patricia | Idea Boutique
041/ 046/ 075/
www.carlitosypatricia.com

ChrisTrivizas | Design
114/
www.christrivizas.eu

Claudia Dionne/Ibo Angulo
002/
www.perrodemundo.com

Clay McIntosh Creative
066/
claymcintosh.com

CUBO DISEÑO
060/ 167/
cubo.es

David Silvosa | Arquitectura & Diseño
176/
www.davidsilvosa.com

Demetrio Mancini
117/
www.demetriomancini.it

Design By Alpha
034/
designbyalpha.com

Design LSC
103/ 132/
designlsc.com

Diseño Cdroig
168/
cdroig.com

Dorian
073/ 078/ 096/
www.estudiodorian.com

Dúctil
020/
www.ductilct.com

Edgar Bak
061/ 139/
www.edgarbak.info

El Cuartel
047/ 077/ 094/ 151/ 152/
elcuartel.es

El Paso, Galería de Comunicación
107/
www.elpasocomunicacion.com

EP designworks
025/
epdesignworks.com

ESIETE
033/ 072/
www.esiete.com

Esther Barniol / Projectes Creatius
016/ 026/ 089/ 102/ 106
estherbarniol.com

estudio eckert+zúñiga
019/ 125/
www.estudio-ez.com

extra!
063/
www.extraestudio.com

Fabien Barral
084/ 178/
www.fabienbarral.com

Firebelly Design
028/
firebellydesign.com

Flatland Design
043/ 049/
www.flatland-design.pt

Flou Flou - disoñadores asociados
006/ 136
www.flouflou.es

Fluid
143/ 163/
fluidesign.co.uk

Foreign Policy Design Group
004/ 157/
www.foreignpolicydesign.com

gestocomunicación
070/
gestocomunicacion.com

Gorka Aizpurua Serrano
037/ 062/ 085/ 166/
www.gorkaizpurua.com

H2D2, Visual Communications
092/
www.h2d2.de

Soon in Tokyo
149/ 179/
www.soonintokyo.com

SOPA Graphics
045/
www.sopagraphics.com

Sophia Georgopoulou
076/
www.sophiag.com

Studio International
127/ 131/ 172/
www.studio-international.com

StudioCentro Marketing srl
059/
www.studiocentromarketing.it

Sublima Comunicación
010/ 048/
www.sublimacomunica.com

SVIDesign
119/
www.svidesign.com

take off - media services
042/ 044/
www.takeoff-ks.de

Tangent Graphic
022/ 177/
www.tangentgraphic.co.uk

The Creative Method
058/ 067/ 105/
www.thecreativemethod.com

The Pencil Factory
121/
www.thepencilfactory.org

Toben
017/ 115/ 116/
toben.com.au

Trapped in Suburbia
003/ 023/ 100/
www.trappedinsuburbia.com

uauh! comunicación gráfica
021/
uauh.es

TwoPoints.Net
057/
www.twopoints.net

Uniform
050/
www.uniform.net

UVE DISEÑO Y COMUNICACION, S.L.
031/ 082/ 159/ 160/
www.estudiouve.com

Valladares Diseño y Comunicación
079/
www.valladaresdc.net

Vellut
053/
www.vellut.cat

Versátil
024/ 122/
www.grupoversatil.com

Vertigo Graphix
051/
www.vertigographix.com

Virbia
112/
www.virbia.com

VisioGlobal
108/ 123
www.visioglobal.com

Zigurat Comunicación Gráfica, S.L.
038/
www.ziguratcomunicacion.es

ZORRAQUINO
036/
www.zorraquino.com